I
WONDER
DISCARDED

I Wonder

Engaging a Child's Curiosity about the Bible

Elizabeth F. Caldwell

Abingdon Press™

Nashville

I WONDER:
ENGAGING A CHILD'S CURIOSITY ABOUT THE BIBLE

This book is printed on acid-free paper.

Library of Congress Cataloging-in-Publication Data

Names: Caldwell, Elizabeth, 1948- author.
Title: I wonder : engaging a child's curiosity about the Bible / Elizabeth F. Caldwell.
Description: First [edition]. | Nashville, Tennessee : Abingdon Press, 2016.
| Includes bibliographical references.
Identifiers: LCCN 2015040330 (print) | LCCN 2015042782 (ebook) | ISBN 9781426799921 (binding: pbk.) | ISBN 9781426799938 (e-book)
Subjects: LCSH: Christian education of children. | Bible--Study and teaching.
Classification: LCC BV1475.3 .C34 2016 (print) | LCC BV1475.3 (ebook) | DDC 248.8/45--dc23
LC record available at http://lccn.loc.gov/2015040330

16 17 18 19 20 21 22 23 24 25—10 9 8 7 6 5 4 3 2 1
MANUFACTURED IN THE UNITED STATES OF AMERICA

Contents

Acknowledgments

Some Thank-Yous and *Dayenu*

I'm grateful to the groups that invited me to teach them, presenting material that I was working on for this book. Thanks to the folks I engaged with here in the Nashville area at Hillsboro Presbyterian Church; First Presbyterian, Franklin; and the Middle Tennessee Presbytery educational gathering. Thanks also to the adults I met with at The Church of the Resurrection Leadership Institute in Kansas City, the Eastern Region of Educators of the Association of Presbyterian Church Educators, and those who participated in The Main Event of Sheppards and Lapsley Presbytery in Birmingham, Alabama.

Thanks to the students at McCormick Theological Seminary and Vanderbilt Divinity School, whose creativity, imagination, and commitments to reading the Bible with children so they get don't have to unlearn things later in life has inspired me to write this book.

Dayenu is sung at the Jewish celebration of Passover. It means "it would have been enough." Thanks to my friend and Old Testament colleague at McCormick Theological Seminary, Ted Hiebert. It would have been enough if you had translated Genesis 11:1-9 in ways that help us see how all the difference in the world as a part of God's plan for us to live together. But you also agreed that we should teach a course together, Reading the Bible with Children, so theological students preparing to be pastors and church leaders could model good biblical scholarship with children. *Dayenu!*

And thanks to my dear friend and colleague Sarah Tanzer. It would have been enough if you had only put up with my questions about Jewish traditions, and you even bought "Protestant" bagels for me (blueberry), but in teaching with you I learned how to read the New Testament in ways that don't include negative stereotypes of Jews, how to read the New Testament without prejudice, to hear how the text would have been heard by its original Jewish and Gentile audience. *Dayenu!*

Jack Seymour and Margaret Ann Crain are both friends and colleagues in the field of religious education. Margaret Ann reminds me that to write well I need to take breaks to work on one quilt square each day. Jack has supported my writing and research since he joined my doctoral committee over twenty-five years ago. I am grateful for his helpful and careful reading and editing of this book. It would have been enough if the two of you had only been good colleagues, but over shared meals in many places in Chicago you also listened, encouraged, and supported me. *Dayenu!*

My sister, Cathy Caldwell Hoop, has always supported my writing with wonderful stories of children. Now she is a pastor serving God's people in Tuscaloosa, Alabama, with her prophetic gifts of compassion, courage, and love. I have learned much about how to engage children's curiosities about Bible stories as I have watched her teach and preach with all God's children of every age. It would have been enough if you had just been my sister but you have also been my patient teacher. *Dayenu!*

And finally, to my husband, Harold Jackson, it would have been enough if you had listened to this book in all of its stages of research and writing, but you also surrounded me with the creative loving space that made this work possible. For your presence in my life and your abounding love I am always grateful. You are the wind beneath my wings. *Dayenu!*

Introduction

I wonder as I wander out under the sky
How Jesus the Saviour did come for to die.

John Jacob Niles, a folksinger, first heard these words sung by a traveling evangelist, Annie Morgan, in 1933, in North Carolina.[1] He memorized them and sang them as a new hymn for Christmas. The words of the hymn capture the story of the birth of Jesus but begin with the end of the story, which is a very interesting way to tell it. Also interesting is how it is told with a wondering question.

Children participate in church educational programs and learn many Bible stories. They possess a lot of factual knowledge about Moses and Miriam, Abraham and Sarah, David, the stories of Jesus and the people he met, and the beginnings of the church, which are told in Acts and the Epistles. Such learning is an important building block in their spiritual formation.

THE CHANCE TO WONDER ABOUT THE BIBLE AS THEY WANDER THROUGH THEIR LIFE IS ESSENTIAL FOR A CHILD'S SPIRITUAL FORMATION, FOR DEVELOPING A LANGUAGE OF FAITH.

Like us, and like John Jacob Niles, children have very important questions about the biblical texts, about the variety of faith expressions they experience in congregations, and about the comments other children make to them as well as the ones they overhear from us. Equally important is the chance for them to ask their own questions about biblical texts, to wonder about the story, to reflect on how they understand and interpret it and the meaning it has for their life. This chance for children to engage the Bible with all their curiosity and questions as they wander through their life is essential for their spiritual formation, for their developing a language of faith. It is incomplete if it only happens in the church. As good as such ministries are, they are insufficient unless supported by parents and families at home.

Contemporary Challenges

As I write this book, the Pew Research Center has released its most recent report on the religious landscape in the United States. Their latest survey of more than 35,000 Americans shows that adults over the age of eighteen who identify themselves as Christians has dropped 8 percent in seven years, while those who identify themselves as unaffiliated religiously (atheist, agnostic, or "nothing in particular") has increased by 6 percent.

A major factor in this decline is those who identify themselves as Christian and the growth of the "nones." The millennial generation (ages eighteen to twenty-four) has less connection with church. "Fully 36% of young Millennials (those between the ages of 18 and 24) are religiously unaffiliated, as are 34% of older Millennials (ages 25-33). And fewer than six-in-ten Millennials identify with any branch of Christianity, compared with seven-in-ten or more among older generations, including Baby Boomers and Gen-Xers."[2]

As smaller churches close and as an older generation dies, many churches across denominations are not seeing growth in membership from the Millenials. The Pew survey reveals that 68 percent say they believe in God, while 37 percent describe themselves as "spiritual" but not "religious," and 21 percent say that prayer is a part of their daily life. They do think that congregations are important in the culture because of the commitments to strengthening bonds with the community and in mission and service with the poor. "With few exceptions, though, the unaffiliated say they are *not* looking for a religion that would be right for them. Overwhelmingly, they think that religious organizations are too concerned with money and power, too focused on rules and too involved in politics."[3]

Another statistic to add to this conversation comes from Mark Chaves whose research has documented the decline in belief by Christians in the literal truth of the Bible. As a sociologist of religion, Chaves has also seen how, along with the decline in belief in biblical inerrancy, there is evidence of growth in Christians' appreciation of religious traditions different from their own. "Even in the midst of high levels of religious belief and practice in American society, there is declining confidence in the special status of one's own religion. No longer seeing the Bible as inerrant is part of a more general shift, even among practicing Christians, away from seeing Christianity as uniquely true."[4]

The Barna Group has published their own findings about the Bible. In 2014 their research indicated six trends for 2014:

1. Skepticism about the Bible has grown and equals the numbers of those who read the Bible at least four times a week.
2. Most Americans do continue to be "pro-Bible," viewing it and its teachings positively. Eighty-seven percent report owning a Bible, and there are at least four Bibles in these households. The most interesting statistic is that 37 percent read the Bible at least once a week.
3. One of the things that keep people from reading the Bible is the busyness of life, which distracts from regular engagement.
4. Electronic versions of the Bible has made it possible for 26 percent to read it more, because of being able to download it on a phone or tablet.
5. People still read the Bible, seeking both answers and comfort.
6. There is less connection in people's beliefs that moral decline in the culture is linked to a lack of reading the Bible.[5]

The implications of this current research for our thinking about how we read the Bible with children are staggering. Pastors, religious educators, and lay leaders have noticed the changing demographics in declining

Sabbath practices of worship and church school participation. Sporadic participation once or twice a month is more the norm than consistent weekly attendance. Church leaders also know the realities of the questions that members bring to the Bible as they seek to understand these ancient texts in light of contemporary cultural challenges. Pastors also hear "confessions" from individuals about the infrequency of their engagement with the Bible and how they want to get into a regular practice of reading the Bible. And, we watch as parents' worldviews about faith and religion shift when they attend interfaith weddings, or watch as their adult children convert to another faith tradition or become "religiously ambiguous" or a "none" (unaffiliated with any religious organization—"none of the above").

What church leaders have been noticing for the last ten years is now being documented by researchers of religion. We are not surprised! We know that when we preach, the introduction to where we are in the text and background about the setting and the character is essential information to share, because without it, many will be unaware. Reminding people of connections between stories in the Gospels is important because many haven't read those stories in a very long time. If children are present in worship and hearing the text read, they may know more than their parents.

THE CHILDREN IN OUR SPIRITUAL CARE NEED A WAY TO ENGAGE THE BIBLE THAT WILL GROW WITH THEM. THEY NEED TO HAVE A SPIRITUAL FOUNDATION WITH THE BIBLE THAT IS GROUNDED AT HOME AS WELL AS IN THE CHURCH.

The reality of all this research is important, because the children in our spiritual care need a way to engage the Bible that will grow with them. They need to have a biblical tool kit that will help them as they bring their questions, the things they wonder about, to the Bible. They need to have a spiritual foundation with the Bible that is grounded at home as well as in the church.

Focus of This Book

This book will address timeless questions such as: how to read and understand the Bible, how to select a Bible, how to understand difficult texts, and how to read ancient texts and interpret their meaning in a contemporary context. Helping children and youth learn new ways of reading and interpreting biblical texts will hopefully help them experience the Bible as both accessible and relevant to their lives of faith.

Chapter 1 asks the question, What story does the Bible tell? It invites those who want to read the Bible with children to consider why and how we do that. Chapter 2 addresses the topic of how children engage the Bible. Readers are invited to consider a wondering model of reading that supports children's spiritual formation. Chapter 3 considers criteria to use in selecting Bibles or Bible storybooks for children and youth. It also provides examples of positive and negative ways to tell and illustrate Bible stories for children.

Persons of every age wrestle with difficult texts in the Bible. Some parents would prefer their children not read about the rape of Dinah in Genesis 34. And we probably all wrestle with the story of the binding of Isaac in Genesis 22. And who doesn't read the book of Jonah and wonder what this story is really about? And we come to the New Testament and read how Jesus welcomes all, especially women, children, and those who seek healing, and those on the fringes of the community. We learn how he taught with parables and, by his actions, how we are to love God and our neighbor. Chapter 4 considers the topic of how we bridge the gap between what we (clergy and educators) have figured out about the Bible and its interpretation and how that knowledge and experience is made available to parents of children.

The last chapter addresses the practical question of how the church can support parents and families in helping their children wonder about the Bible. What should we be teaching children and youth about the Bible? What experiences with the Bible should we be offering them?

THE APPROACH TO ENGAGING THE BIBLE USED IN THIS BOOK INVITES THE READER TO USE *SOFT EYES*. SOFT EYES ENABLE A PERSON TO SEE WIDER.

The approach to engaging the Bible used in this book invites the reader to use *soft eyes*. Soft eyes is an expression taken from *Akido*, the Japanese art of self-defense. With soft eyes, you have whole vision, not partial. In *Akido,* two kinds of eyes have been found to be responsive when a person is taken by surprise. A hard eye narrows vision, shutting out the periphery so as to respond to the perceived fight or fear. Soft eyes provides a contrast, opening wide the periphery so that a person can take in more of the world. So instead of responding to a threat or to the world with a narrow tunnel vision, soft eyes enable a person to see wider.

Educator Parker Palmer has written about this concept in his book, *The Courage to Teach: Exploring the Inner Landscape of a Teacher's Life.* "Soft eyes, it seems to me is an evocative image for what happens when we gaze on sacred reality. Now our eyes are open and receptive, able to take in the greatness of the world and the grace of great things. Eyes wide with wonder we no longer need to resist or run when taken by surprise. Now we can open ourselves to the great mystery."[6]

How we read and interpret the Bible with children may mean the difference between whether or not it will continue to be an important source for their life of faith as they become young adults. Do we read it in fear, afraid of what is there and what children might think, and what questions they may ask us about it? Does our own fear keep us from opening our eyes wide with softness to the possibilities for hearing and seeing God's activity in the past with God's people and even today with all those whom God loves?

TEACHING CHILDREN HOW TO READ AND INTERPRET THE BIBLE IN WAYS THAT THEY DON'T HAVE TO UNLEARN LATER IS ESSENTIAL.

Teaching children how to read and interpret the Bible in ways that they don't have to unlearn later is essential. Remembering to read the Bible, wondering about the stories and inviting children to engage with their questions and imagination, will contribute to their faith formation. This book will be a resource for adults (parents, pastors, educators, church school teachers) who want to explore ways to help children read, engage, and wrestle with the Bible honestly, directly, and faithfully. This book will be a resource for those who come to the Bible with souls open to be fed and who want to grow with children in their biblical and theological wisdom.

CHAPTER ONE

What Story Does the Bible Tell?

When I write for children about the spiritual, I strive to create such stories, stories that use language in ways that are clear, filled with metaphor and symbolic images, concrete and personally relevant to children's experiences, and open to ongoing questions and conversations. I imagine that these kinds of narratives have the capacity to help our youth and children grow up. Whether or not they are literally true, good stories have the power to help us better understand who we are and what we believe.

—Rabbi Sandy Eisenberg Sasso

"Jesus loves me this I know, for the Bible tells me so." This familiar childhood song reminds us of a basic theological concept. It's in the Gospel stories where we first hear and learn about Jesus. Moreover, we learn about love as it is first experienced at home in relationship with family members. We connect the love spoken about Jesus with our experiences of being loved by those around us. Beyond singing this beloved song with its simple affirmation of faith, what else are children learning about the Bible?

Why We Tell the Story of the Bible and Our Hopes in Keeping This Story Alive with Our Children

From 2002 to 2005, The National Study of Youth and Religion interviewed more than three thousand American teenagers (ages thirteen to seventeen) and found that a majority of youth reflect the religious faith of their parents. In this study, Melinda Lundquist Denton and Christian

Smith discovered that mainline Protestant youth who attended church with their parents were "among the least religiously articulate of all teens."[1] They found that the youth they interviewed were inarticulate with regard to speaking about their faith "because no one had taught them how to talk about their faith, or provided opportunities to practice using a faith vocabulary."[2]

A faith vocabulary is first shared and practiced at home as parents and other family members raise a child in the Christian faith. Reading the Bible, becoming familiar with its stories and the themes that are woven throughout is one of the most important ways for children to learn a vocabulary of faith.

READING THE BIBLE IS ONE OF THE MOST IMPORTANT WAYS FOR CHILDREN TO LEARN A VOCABULARY OF FAITH.

In their reflection on The National Study of Youth and Religion study and its implications for the religious lives of teenagers, Smith and Denton identified several conclusions that are important for our thinking about the role of parents in the religious formation of their children. They found that parents have the most influence in the religious and spiritual formation of their teenage children: "The best social predictor, although not a guarantee, of what the religious and spiritual lives of youth will look like is what the religious and spiritual lives of their parents *do* look like.... Parents, will most likely, 'get what they are.'"[3]

A second important conclusion from the study is finding that many US teenagers have a very difficult time articulating what they believe or the ways their belief systems impact their daily lives. "Religion seems very much a part of the lives of many U.S. teenagers, but for most of them it is in ways that seem quite unfocused, implicit, in the background, just part of the furniture... important but not a priority, valued but not much invested in, praised but not very describable."[4]

In this book that focuses on how we read the Bible with children, these conclusions about teenagers are worth remembering. The faith that teenagers exhibit is the result of what they experience in the home. What is modeled for them by their parents is most important. And the ways that faith and practices of faith impact the everyday, such as reading the Bible and connecting biblical stories with living life on a daily basis, means the difference in their ability to articulate what they believe and how they will live. Will their faith be one that can be articulated in words and actions or will it be decorative, "just part of the furniture," easily rearranged, moved to the background or storage?

Rabbi Sandy Eisenberg Sasso believes that children need a language of faith and it begins with story, "because that's how children make sense of their world through narrative and story." Sasso states,

> I think such language also comes through ritual and experience. The earliest spiritual experiences that children have often come through routine and ritual that are repeated over and over again. And often when I speak to children and I ask them when do they feel the presence of God, or if they could point to a particular experience, they often speak of rituals or moments where they felt very close to their parents and it helped them give expression to what they were feeling.[5]

There is an intimacy present when stories are shared. When parents tell or read a Bible story with a child they are making a commitment of time and space to share in their child's spiritual growth. In the telling and reading of stories, in the pauses for questions and comments that always arise, parents are making their spiritual life open and near to their child. And in this intimacy of sharing and wondering together, both child and parent grow together spiritually.

CHILDREN NEED A LANGUAGE OF FAITH AND IT BEGINS WITH STORY.

Methodist pastor Kenda Creasy Dean, writing in her book, *Almost Christian: What the Faith of Our Teenagers Is Telling the American Church*, contrasts a "diner theology" of "being nice, feeling good about yourself and saving God for emergencies" with a "consequential faith, which is far more likely to take root in the rich relational soil of families, congregations, and mentor relationships where young people can see what faithful lives look like, and encounter the people who love them enacting a larger story of divine care and hope."[6]

One of the ways that children become adults who are theologically articulate is to have experiences with the Bible, a foundation of faith for Christians. In his book *The Strange Silence of the Bible in the Church* (1970), James D. Smart noted the importance of lay people engaging in Bible study, although only 5 percent of congregations actually do so. Smart commented on the reasons why 95 percent feel no need for this kind of study.

> Their version of the Christian faith and the Christian life is of a character that they can dispense with any serious delving into the scripture. They are content with a church in which all things are done decently and in order, which makes minimal demands upon their time and provides a maximum of moral stability and spiritual security for them and for the immediate community in which they live.... They are too confident of their ability to remain faithful to Jesus Christ while ignorant of the Scriptures that witness to him.[7]

Forty years separate these quotes by Dean and Smart! Yet the similarity of their observations is astounding—perhaps a wake-up call for those who are interested in raising their children in faithful Christian homes. Practicing the faith at home can be done in many ways. John Westerhoff, an Episcopalian religious educator, wrote a very practical book in 1980 titled *Bringing Up Children in the Christian Faith.* In it he suggests five guidelines for sharing faith with children from birth through childhood. He believes that it is the responsibility of parents and family members to help children grow up with a language and an experience of faith. This is possible when children hear and read and recall stories from the Bible. Children grow in their faith when they learn how to pray—at meals and bedtime—and how to offer prayers for others. Westheroff believes that the Christian faith is first experienced by children when they see how the things they do for others—like listening, helping those in need, caring for someone who needs help—are important activities of service. And children's faith is supported by their participation in the life of a congregation as they learn to worship, celebrate the church seasons, participate in the sacraments, and know that there is a family called church who loves them.[8]

Similarly, Daniel Aleshire, a religious educator who is now the head of the Association of Theological Schools, wrote this definition of Christian education:

> Christian education involves those tasks and expressions of ministry that enable people (1) to learn the Christian story, both ancient and present; (2) to develop the skills they need to act out their faith; (3) to reflect on that story in order to live self-aware to its truth; and (4) to nurture the sensitivities they need to live together as a covenant community.[9]

The first guideline, learning and telling the story, is the focus of this book. In some ways it may be the hardest one for many parents. Questions abound:

- What stories do we read together?
- Where do we begin?
- What if they ask questions I can't answer?
- I'm not sure what I believe about the Bible, so how do I read the Bible with my child?

Sources for these questions and apprehensions about reading the Bible with children focus on a variety of issues.

1. Previous Experience with the Bible

If you grew up attending church school as a child, then you may have a memory bank of favorite stories, probably stories of familiar biblical characters from the Hebrew Bible: Adam and Eve, Noah, Sarah and Abraham, Ruth and Naomi, David, Esther, Jonah. You may also know a lot of the stories of Jesus (birth, life, teachings, death and resurrection) and some stories of the early church and its leaders: Paul, Peter, Timothy. Or you may have forgotten a lot.

And if you did not grow up in a religious tradition or if your family was only nominally Christian, attending church on Christmas and Easter, then your lack of experience with the Bible may be an obstacle to reading it with a child.

2. Knowledge and Level of Comfort with Reading and Studying the Bible

If you have a lot of knowledge about biblical stories, perhaps they are like beads strung on a necklace—each one there as a separate entity yet connected because of being important parts of the one story of the Bible, the story of God's love for humankind.

If you have continued in your own reading and study of the Bible, both individually and with groups in your congregation, then you have had the chance to grow in your understanding of biblical text and learn more about these stories and how they fit together.

Continuing to read and study means that the stories you read as a child or youth may now be understood in new ways. For example, the story of Noah and the flood, a vivid reminder of the relationship between God and God's creation and the first time we hear the word *covenant*, can be understood as a universal story of loss and recovery. Who can't relate to that ancient story when you consider your own experiences of loss and recovery and God's abiding presence?

3. Current Challenges and Practices

Most homes abound with copies of different Bible translations. Are they on the shelf? Is there a favorite that is read? Do children ever see a parent open or read the Bible? Have you given up on reading it because it is not easily understood?

These kinds of experiences in the past and current practices provide the background for considering how to begin again with a child. What in the past experience of parents needs to be held on to and affirmed as a good building block for nurturing a child's growth as a Christian? What in the past needs to be let go so that some new practices of faith can emerge?

How can a vocabulary of faith for both parent and child grow as they engage the Bible together?

Craig Dykstra, former vice president of religion for Lilly Endowment, has written that it is imperative that we help youth recover a religious language that is "clear enough to be comprehended by young people, rich enough to be meaningful, concrete enough to relate to the world as it is, and critical enough to keep open the dynamics of inquiry and continuing conversation."[10] One of the ways this religious language is supported is through engagement with the Bible, that holy book that informs us and acts on us. Dykstra has said that "God is using the Bible not only to inform us but to form us and reform us, to shape us into God's own."[11] Dean asks this question of parents, "Do we practice the kind of faith we want our children to have?"[12] So before we begin to consider how we read the Bible with our children, it's important to begin with ourselves and our beliefs and assumptions.

Why We Read the Bible

Take a minute and consider your response to these open-ended sentences:

The Bible is...

The Bible is not...

My own experience with reading the Bible is...

When I read the Bible, I struggle with...

A question I have about the Bible is...

Dykstra's question about how we are being formed, informed, and reformed by our reading of the Bible is a great place to begin. Often I begin a workshop for parents and grandparents with this question: What experiences of reading the Bible did you grow up with as a child? The answers have become fairly predictable. A majority say they grew up with nothing in the home. Some remember a favorite Bible storybook that they read. One or two remember a parent or grandparent who told them

Bible stories from memory. Few are able to remember ever seeing a parent reading the Bible.

Bible storybooks often include an opening statement about the Bible. These statements provide clues for parents about the hopes and purposes for inviting children into the stories. As you read these statements, what do you notice? What is most explicit about the statement about the Bible? What is more implicit or assumed? Is there anything missing, something you wished had been said?

- *Shine On: A Story Bible* says in the introduction, "For Christians, the Bible is a rare and precious treasure, an inspiration and guide for our lives. It is a place where we come to listen to God." In describing the variety of kinds of writing contained in the Bible, it says: "These stories present anew the exciting, curious, wonderful account of a God at work in the world with flawed, genuine people. They inspire children and adults to discuss, question and act in response to the biblical message."[13]

- In the *Children of God Storybook Bible,* Desmond Tutu reminds children that God wants us to love others and that is accomplished when we do three things: "Do what is RIGHT, be KIND TO ONE ANOTHER, and be FRIENDS WITH GOD. You will see these teachings and many more in God's stories, which we have gathered here for you and all of God's children."[14]

- The *Candle Read and Share Bible* includes a letter to parents in the beginning. "What you are holding in your hands is not just a book; it's a unique way to share God's Word with the children in your life, a way to help them come to know God's love, goodness, and faithfulness to us . . . and to share that good news with others."[15]

- In *The Jesus Storybook Bible, Every Story Whispers His Name*, the author addresses two assumptions readers often make about the Bible, that it is a book of rules or it is a book about heroes. "The Bible is most of all a story . . . one Big Story. The Story of how God loves his children and comes to rescue them. It takes the whole Bible to tell this Story. And at the center of the Story, there is a baby. Every Story in the Bible whispers his name."[16]

- *The Pilgrim Book of Bible Stories* divides the selected stories it includes into nineteen chapters, "each has an introduction that reveals the developing thread of the story, linking history to interpretation, literature to life. This approach roots the stories in the historical reality of their times."[17]

- *The Mystic Bible* by Alexandra Sangster is a collection of stories of Jesus that begins with his birth and concludes with Pentecost. It is advertised on the progressive Christianity website as using inclusive language to tell "the ancient stories of love" through text, poetry, and illustrations.

- *The Deep Blue Kids Bible*, which is the Common English Bible translation, includes age-appropriate notes for children. The editors remind the readers that "the Bible is more than just a big book. It's a gift to us from God! It's also a gift to us from many people. It took hundreds of years and thousands of people to bring us this gift. And like all good gifts, this Bible is meant to be opened, explored, and enjoyed. It's our hope that you will learn more about God, the Bible, Jesus, faith, and how it all fits into life today."[18]

We see how different storybooks introduce the Bible to children as "one big story," a book that is a "gift to us from God," a love story from God, a collection of different kinds of stories written by people a long time ago, a "precious treasure, an inspiration and guide for our lives. It is a place where we come to listen to God."

HEARING THE BIBLE STORIES IN RELATIONSHIP WITH LOVING PARENTS OR FAMILY MEMBERS FORMS CHILDREN IN FAITH AND HELPS THEM DEVELOP A LANGUAGE OF FAITH THAT WILL GROW WITH THEM.

Church school and midweek programs are great places where children can learn about the Bible and God's love for them as they have the opportunity to engage in the stories and see the connections the text has to their lives. Even more important than these formal settings for learning are the informal opportunities to hear the stories and wonder about their meanings as they hear the Bible told and read to them at home. Hearing the Bible stories in relationship with loving parents or family members forms children in faith and helps them develop a language of faith, a faith vocabulary that will grow with them.

How Do We Read the Bible with Children?

A commitment to reading the Bible with children requires that we do so with a critical lens. Bible storybooks seem to share a common canon of stories that are included. Stories with animals or fish, stories of female and male heroes in the Old Testament, and stories of Jesus are always included. When we introduce children to these stories for the first time, we do so knowing that they will continue to hear and read them repeatedly over the course of their childhood if they are active participants in the educational life of a congregation. How the stories are told matters. Just like we choose what stories from our families we share and when we share them, we also need to make this decision when we teach stories from the Bible to our children.

Reading for More than Information

In her chapter, "The Word Became Visual Text: The Boy Jesus in Children's Bibles" in *Text, Image, Otherness in Children's Bibles, What is the Picture?*, Melody Briggs contrasts two ways that biblical stories can be told in children's Bibles. When the text is tamed so as to get a "certain outcome in the reader" then,

> The text becomes a didactic tool, and narrative takes second place to function. . . . When children's Bibles present the biblical text as a source of information or training, readers may be led to think, "I know that information or moral. I don't need to read it again." For readers to experience the text

> in such a way that they want to return to it, children's Bibles need to draw readers into the biblical world and leave them wanting to visit there again.[19]

Several Bible storybooks provide good examples of these two ways of reading biblical texts. The story of Jonah, the prophet who was sent by God to tell the Ninevites they needed to change the ways they were living, is a popular story to include in children's Bible storybooks because of the big fish. In fact, many title it "Jonah and the Big Fish." And colorful illustrations of Jonah inside the fish are often included.

As we know from reading this story, it's not a story about a big fish. It is a story about God and God's prophet, Jonah, and it's a story about how God loved the people of Nineveh. So to title it "Jonah and the Big Fish" is an example of how storybooks tame the text. It makes it a nice little story, directing the focus of the children's attention to the fish with Jonah inside it. It's easy then for children to learn this story and think, "Okay, I know that story now, why do I need to read it again?" Taught in this way, they miss the opportunity to engage the story and wonder about the meaning. With their attention diverted to the "big fish" they may not get to the point of the story about God sending a prophet to speak to people who were the prophet's enemies.

In a comparison of seven versions of this story in children's Bible storybooks, four did not include the ending of the story where God finds Jonah after his successful visit to Nineveh. This dialogue between a pouting prophet and God provides an excellent way to engage children in wondering about Jonah, God, and the Ninevites who repented of their ways. When a Bible storybook chooses not include the important ending of the story, like this one, then the text is tamed. When the whole story is told, children are able to grow with the story and their understanding of it. As they grow from concrete thinkers to being able to think more abstractly, then they are able to wrestle with its meaning for their lives and begin to see that rather than a story about a big fish, it is a larger story of running away, of doing bad things, of being forgiven—a story of God's love and kindness. These are all behaviors that children experience. In allowing the story of Jonah to be a narrative that children can engage differently at different age levels, the text is not tamed.

Several versions of the Jonah story do invite children to appreciate the narrative, and hopefully when reading these versions they are encouraged to return to the text again. Perhaps the editors of these storybooks decided to include the whole story because they wanted children to learn about God's love for the outsider and the responsibility for us to reach out.

The *Candle Read and Share Bible* is a great Bible storybook for young children (ages three to five). It divides Jonah into five shorter stories: Jonah Runs Away, A Big Storm, Jonah Goes Overboard, Inside a Big Fish, and Jonah Obeys God. Each story includes a textbox with a comment or a question. The one included in the last story—"Do you think Jonah wished he'd gone to Nineveh the first time?"[20]—invites the children to engage the story with their imaginations, maybe even putting themselves into the character of Jonah.

The Lion Read and Know Bible does a good job of retelling the story and includes colorful illustrations. It's a very thoughtful example of how retelling a biblical story for children can make the narrative both interesting and inviting to children's imaginations. Since the story of Jonah really focuses on God and God's call to the prophet Jonah—and the Ninevites and their response—it can invite even young readers to engage the story from different perspectives and angles of vision. The story of Jonah in this storybook offers children the opportunity to think about the nature of God and God's relationship with humans.

After Jonah gives his message from God to the Ninevites, they realize that God is very angry with them and that they must change their "wicked ways. 'Oh no!' cried the people. 'Disaster!' wept the king. 'We must change at once. We must show God we are sorry. Perhaps God will be kind.' And God was kind."[21]

The author obviously carefully considered how to communicate the behavior of the Ninevites and the response of God in language children could understand. Translating God's forgiving the Ninevites as an act of God's kindness invites children to continue to wrestle with the story and what it means for their life in particular, when they are faced with the challenges represented in this short story.

There is one storybook that interestingly provides an example of both ways of reading. "God's Messenger" is the title for this story, and the first sentence invites children to appreciate the narrative and to want to know more. "God had a job for Jonah. But Jonah didn't want it" is how this story begins in *The Jesus Storybook Bible, Every Story Whispers His Name.* The story is told both creatively with imaginative illustrations and with an accurate retelling that closely follows the text until the ending. The opening sentence provides a great way for a child both to engage his or her curiosity about Jonah and also to connect with ways God might be inviting him or her to do an important job.

The final part of the story when God returns to find Jonah pouting under a wilting shrub is not included; instead there are two paragraphs that connect the story of Jonah to Jesus. "Many years later, God was going to send another Messenger with the same wonderful message. Like Jonah he would spend three days in utter darkness. But this Messenger would be God's own Son."[22] In making the connection between Jonah and Jesus, I think the author tames the text by choosing the outcome for the child. Instead of allowing the child to stay with the story of Jonah and how God invited Jonah to do a difficult job, spending time with people who were his enemies, the author ended the story by asking the child to connect the story with Jesus.

OUR HOPE IN READING THE BIBLE WITH CHILDREN IS THAT ITS STORIES WILL GROW WITH THEM SO THAT READING AND HEARING THE BIBLE BECOMES MORE THAN JUST GAINING INFORMATION.

Our hope in reading with children is that the Bible stories will grow with them. As they hear them and engage them at different points in their life, hopefully they will hear the story in new ways and so their reading and hearing of stories from the Bible becomes more than just gaining information. Continuing engagement with the story invites reflection on the text, which is an essential foundation for faithful living as a Christian.

Taming the Text or Not

The Bibles that we read and use at home and church are based on the work of translators who carefully study the scriptures in their original languages, such as Hebrew and Greek. It is always interesting to study biblical texts with groups in the church and to hear a story or verse read from different translations. Hearing Psalm 23 read from the King James Version, New Revised Standard Version, New International Version, Common English Bible, or from a paraphrase such as *The Message* by Eugene Peterson is a great way to see how translations differ, how meaning changes when the same word is translated in different versions.

Children's Bible storybooks will disclose in the opening pages the particular translation on which the stories are based. Sometimes the author will provide more information about her or his angle of vision in an introduction. A majority of storybooks leave the discovery up to the reader. Briggs describes these stories rewritten for children as

> an echo of the text, an interpretation that determines the form of the biblical text provided to children. Their production is generally guided by two aims: to communicate biblical content to children, rather than actual words of Scripture, and to make the text relevant to its target readers.[23]

In addition to choosing what stories to include, writers of Bible storybooks for children also focus on the structure of the story and how it is designed to communicate a particular meaning, thus eliminating other meanings from being considered.[24] Briggs identifies four approaches used in retelling Bible stories for children. When a story is written so as to communicate a particular moral, it can be labeled *value driven.* The author wants to connect the story very explicitly to the life of the child. The classic example of this can be found in older children's Bible storybooks in the story of Jesus as a child when he left his parents and was found in the temple reading with the religious leaders. When the story concludes with a nice summary for children to obey their parents, then the larger meanings of the story are eliminated so as to make the story a moral lesson for children.

Similarly some authors or editors of Bible storybooks believe that children need to be protected from incorrect thinking and so the story, either in its retelling or in a sidebar note, provides a theological boundary for the child. This approach to storytelling is *dogma driven*. The story of Jonah from *The Jesus Storybook Bible, Every Story Whispers His Name* is an example of this kind of approach. By connecting the story of Jonah to the story of Jesus, the author provides a frame or boundary for the story. The story is not allowed to stand on its own but provides a strong connection for the child to make between Jonah and Jesus, a connection that is not explicit in the text. Both of these approaches tame the text, making it fit a particular teaching or moral that is deemed important and appropriate by the storyteller.

Two additional approaches are examples of stories that are written to guide the child who is reading them. When a biblical story is supplemented with additional information or dialogue, it is considered to be *education driven*. And finally some storytellers want the story to invite the reader's curiosity and imagination, keep the ambiguity of the text alive, encourage the child to wrestle with it, ask questions, wonder about it, and even resolve it. Stories written in this style are *engagement driven*.[25]

These four approaches to storytelling for children (value driven, dogma driven, education driven, and engagement driven) can easily be found in the story of Mary and Martha and how it is retold in four storybooks. This story of the sisters who entertained Jesus in their home is included in most children's Bible storybooks. It's a good example of how biblical text can be read and interpreted and how interpretation can either tame the text or invite additional wonderings about its meaning both for the cultural context in which it was told and for readers today.

The story is told simply in Luke 10:38-42. When Jesus is welcomed into their home in Galilee, Mary sits at his feet, listening to Jesus talk while Martha "was preoccupied with getting everything ready for their meal." When Martha complained to Jesus about all the work she was doing by herself, Jesus responded to her that she was worried and distracted, and that Mary had chosen the better thing to do. "It won't be taken away from her."

Biblical scholars help us understand this text by providing information that adds texture to this simple story. When we read that Mary sat at Jesus's feet, it was not just a physical action but more than that. It meant that in doing so, she was sitting to learn from Jesus's teaching. So while Mary was listening to Jesus, we read that Martha was more concerned about getting the meal on the table and was getting no help from her sister with the preparations. Martha thought she was right in expressing her frustration to Jesus, whom she may have assumed would support her.

Instead Jesus made two observations. He told Martha that she was worried and distracted trying to get the meal ready. And then he said, "One thing is necessary." Mary had chosen well, to sit, listen, and learn. And then the second observation from Jesus was directed to Mary, about whom he said, the part she had chosen would not be taken from her.

Biblical scholars remind us of the importance of this story both for the cultural world of those for whom this story was written and for readers today. When Mary chose to "sit at Jesus's feet," she chose a role that had been traditionally one available to men. And Martha, who complained to Jesus thinking that of course he would back her up, did just the opposite. Jesus invited Martha to look at what she was doing, to think about why she was *distracted*—a Greek word for being pulled in many different directions. And Jesus affirmed what Mary had chosen to do, to take the role of a learner, to be a disciple.

With this background, let's look at how the story is told in selected children's Bible storybooks and how they illustrate four approaches to reading and understanding. *For Such a Time as This: Stories of Women from the Bible, Retold for Girls* includes texts based on the Holman Christian Standard Bible and the English Standard Version. Here the story is given the title, "The One Thing, The Story of Mary and Martha and the Dinner." The story follows the text, adding in dialogue that amplifies Martha's frustration with Mary's decision to sit and listen to Jesus's teaching. "Mary became frustrated at the way her sister Mary was lazily sitting on the ground while Martha was busy working. 'Jesus,' Martha said, 'don't you care that my sister has left me to do all this work alone?' Her voice was as sharp as a knife, and she wanted Him to do something about the situation."[26]

One of the common practices of children's Bible stories is to fill in the gaps of the text. Details in the story about what Mary was thinking are added: "But the truth was that Mary recognized how amazing it was to be in the presence of Jesus, and she couldn't imagine any of the other tasks when she could simply soak up His wisdom. Her heart was filled to the brim as she worshipped the Lord, and she knew that all the other duties could wait."[27]

The phrase "simply soak up" and "her heart was filled to the brim" invite the reader to focus on Mary's emotional reactions to the experience of sitting at Jesus's feet. By filling in the emotional gaps of the character of Mary, this author has tamed the text, turning the story to address important social values. Emphasizing the emotional response of Mary adds texture to the text, focusing the reader's attention to the emotional response of Mary, thus affirming gender stereotyping for girls: boys think and girls feel. It stands in contrast to what could have been done, affirming the simple act of sitting at Jesus's feet as the act of a disciple, what men had been doing for years at the synagogue, evoking a response of intellect and thinking, not emotion.

Each story in this storybook is followed by a page that has three paragraphs. The first, *He*, connects the story to an attribute of God. The second, *Me*, invites the reader to connect their lives with the story, and *She*, the third, is a prayer written for parents focusing on a quality of attribute that is present in the story.

As indicated in the *Me* and *She* paragraphs, the response to the story is clearly written so as to impart the value of respecting God. The child is encouraged to remember what it means to show respect to and honor leaders. The *She* paragraph includes this sentence in the prayer: "When she is tempted to respond with a rebellious spirit, pushing her boundaries and alienating those who lead her, keep her eternal goals in mind, taking care not to nag at her or frustrate her unnecessarily."[28] Both of these sections use the story to impart the value of obedience and respect.

A second approach to the text is dogma driven, where the story is told in such a way to provide a theological boundary as a protection for the reader. The *He* response to the story is a great example of this approach. The quality of God that is selected for connection with this story is jealousy. Girls are reminded that God is a jealous God because "he cannot stand to see us waste our devotion on anything less than Himself."[29]

The author wants a girl to connect the implicit jealousy of Martha for her sister Mary, a fairly common textual interpretation, with the jealous love of God. This is a clear example of how a theological agenda can drive the retelling of a story. Consider how the *He* or *God* section could have been written differently to frame a different theological understanding of God. What if instead of "God is **jealous** in His love for us," the author had written, "God is always inviting us to learn and grow." It changes the view of God.

When Bible stories and reflections for children are written with particular values and dogmas in mind, it's important to be able to recognize them and name them. Such approaches can tame a text but they also have the possibility of opening a text up for new ways of thinking.

Two approaches that guide the reader are evident in several children's story Bibles. Stories that add new information to the biblical text approach it from the need to educate, providing more information. This is the purpose of Ralph Milton in *The Family Story Bible.* In "Mary Learns about Food" the story is told from the point of view of Martha. Rather than ending with the observation about Mary having chosen the better response, Jesus engages Martha in a conversation about food, "It isn't food you eat with your mouth. It is food that helps you grow inside . . . food that feeds us for our whole lives."[30] The story concludes with Jesus talking with Martha about this kind of food that is God's love. "So let's sit and talk for a while. We'll share one kind of food, then after a while, we'll both help you prepare the other kind."

Rather than making the story about the jealousy between the sisters, Milton, by focusing on its retelling from the point of view of Martha, imagines how Jesus might have responded to Martha. His addition to the text provides an imaginative way to invite the reader to think about how

Jesus could have invited Martha to do what her sister had been doing, listening, and learning with Jesus.

For authors who want readers to engage the text, stories are written so as not to fill in all the gaps in the story, to maintain some of the ambiguity, inviting children to bring their own questions, observations, and wonderings to the story. *Shine On: A Story Bible* consistently does the best job of this kind of approach to Bible stories. The story is simply retold from the NRSV, which is the translation used in *Shine On*. Readers are invited to engage it by considering their response to three questions: Wonder, Connect, and Explore. A Wonder question invites children to "Imagine being Martha, trying to do all the work for your guests." The Connect question does a great job of helping children connect both ways of being a disciple, the activity of listening and learning and *diakonia*, the act of serving: "Following Jesus means doing things to help others, and sitting and listening. What kinds of work do we do to help others? How can we quietly listen to God?" Explore invites children to learn more about the cultural world of this text and the roles of women.[31]

What Parents Need: Help with Rearranging the Furniture

The quote from the beginning of this chapter about the faith of teenagers is both revealing and indicting. The National Study of Youth and Religion found that for a majority of teenagers interviewed, there was no vocabulary of faith; faith seemed to be only present in the background of their lives, not really a priority, "just part of the furniture." And they learned this at home.

Obviously, a place to begin is with parents, the ones who have all good commitments as they bring their children to worship to be baptized, the ones who are well intentioned as they drop off their children for church school while they run errands, the ones who believe that one hour a week of Christian education will form their children forever for a life of Christian faith—yes, all of these and more.

APPROACHING THE BIBLE AS AN ADULT, EITHER FOR PERSONAL READING OR FOR READING WITH CHILDREN, IS NOT UNLIKE STAGING A HOME. IT REQUIRES SOME DECLUTTERING, REARRANGING, AND REMOVAL.

I recently moved from Chicago to Nashville. I faced the daunting task of dealing with twenty-five years of living in the same place. Moving experts will tell you that a way to begin as you face stuffed closets is to make three piles: give away, throw away, and keep. That much I knew, but my real estate agent insisted that I work with a stager who would get my condo ready for the competitive market. Mentally I was prepared that she would come in and totally change my beloved home by getting rid of the clutter, all to make it look better for potential buyers. But halfway through the day as I watched a beloved antique chair banished to the basement, I realized staging meant redoing everything: furniture, art work, even taking down a wall of beloved family memories framed in photographs. Through my tears I realized how hard it was to move, to let go of things I loved, to let someone else rearrange my furniture, my stuff. All of this so that strangers could walk into my home and the new arrangement would be pleasing to their eye, not distracting.

Approaching the Bible as an adult, either for personal reading or for reading with children, is not unlike staging a home. It requires some decluttering, rearranging, and removal. So consider these three questions:

Remove—What Assumptions and Past Experiences with the Bible Need to Be Discarded?

A major obstacle for some adults with regard to engaging with the Bible either for themselves or with their children is previous experience. Adults today come to our churches with a variety of religious background. Perhaps they were raised in a tradition where belief in the literal truth of every word in the Bible was required. And if they have rejected that belief, removed it, what has it been replaced with? Now they come searching for a new way of understanding biblical interpretation.

A woman is hesitant to read the Bible anymore. She is tired of the lack of inclusive language and wonders what is redeemable in the Bible. And as a mother she is adamant about wanting a Bible for her daughter that will not teach her things that will have to be unlearned later.

Declutter—What Beliefs about the Bible Do You Hold On to and Why Are They Important?

Maybe a man left the church, graduated from church, as we say, after confirmation, and is now returning with a child. He brings with him his memories of favorite stories from the Bible he learned as a child, Jonah and the big fish, Noah and the flood, the Beatitudes, which he was required to learn for confirmation. He remembers individual stories but wonders what they are truly about and how these ancient stories written for a people in such a different time and culture have meaning for his life today. As he thinks about all of the different kinds of writing in the Bible, he wants to know more so that he can better read the Bible with his children.

Rearrange—What Space and Time Can Be Made for Engaging the Biblical Story?

"I'm too busy right now." "I really don't know enough about the Bible to be a teacher." "I like to keep my weekend options open, so I can't make a weekly commitment." You probably know the question for which these are answers! Yes, it's the invitation to adults to be a teacher in the church school. If you interviewed church school teachers, they would probably tell you they have the same excuses but for some reason they chose to rearrange the furniture of their lives so as to make reading the Bible—and preparing to teach it—a priority.

After the stager left, in defiance I brought the beloved antique chair up from the basement. I refused to take down the quilts that hung on the walls of the hall and I rehung a few of the photographs. After all, I thought, it's still my home for a little while longer and I'm still living here. I need something of the familiar, something of me here, in my home that has just been staged so as to be anonymous.

Fortunately I had two dear friends who offered to be there with me during the daylong process of staging my condo. Obviously they both knew me well and knew more about staging and its impact than I did. My friends didn't comment, criticize, or abandon me. With good humor and the occasional sarcastic comment, they kept me going. They helped me make choices. They packed up stuff for moving and they willingly loaded their car with bags of items to donate to Goodwill. They refused to leave until the stager did. I couldn't have gotten through that day without them.

I learned a lot that day. I learned that I could rise to the challenge of staging. Once I got over the initial shock of everything I had thoughtfully placed being rehung and replaced, I realized my energies taken up with resistance could be better used, so I worked with the stager.

In this personal parable I think pastors and religious educators are like those friends of mine who stayed with me through the agonizing process of dealing with my stuff, surely a symbol for the major changes in my life that had begun. As we preach and teach, as we listen to parents talk about their lives and their lives of faith, we have the opportunity to both challenge and support them as they consider their attitudes, experiences, and priorities for engaging the biblical story.

We challenge them when we invite them to revisit long-held assumptions and attitudes about the Bible. What needs to be kept, what can be removed? We support adults when we invite them to declutter and be willing and open to reading the Bible in new ways, with fresh interpretations and insights for daily living.

And we stand with them as they begin to rearrange thinking and actions so as to make room for engaging the biblical story. We support them with resources and guidance and our presence as they wrestle in new ways with the things they know and the things the Bible tells them are so. We support them by listening as they work to claim new understandings and practices.

Katherine Paterson is a well-known children's author who also writes about her experience of writing for children, which she has been doing for a very long time. She has said that

> we cannot give them [children] what we do not have. We cannot share what we do not care for deeply ourselves. If we prescribe books as medicine, our children have a perfect right to refuse the nasty-tasting spoon. . . . Really good books . . . pull together for us a world that is falling apart. They are the words that integrate us, stretch us, judge us, comfort and heal us. They are the words that mirror the Word of creation, bringing order out of chaos.[32]

Surely faith in our children can be more than background to their lives, when we, as faithful adults, join them in reading, engaging, and reflecting on the Bible and its words and ideas that "stretch us, judge us, comfort us and heal us." In the Bible we meet God. In the Bible God reveals God's self in the teaching and ministry of Jesus and in the improbable and sometimes impossible moments and places in our lives when we know and believe with all our hearts that God's Spirit is there, providing strength, encouragement, and hope. In the Bible we meet people just like ourselves and, like them, we find the resources of faith and belief that help us face life as we remove, declutter, and rearrange what is necessary and required for our belief systems.

SURELY FAITH IN OUR CHILDREN CAN BE MORE THAN BACKGROUND TO THEIR LIVES, WHEN WE, AS FAITHFUL ADULTS, JOIN THEM IN READING, ENGAGING, AND REFLECTING ON THE BIBLE.

Katherine Paterson is correct. We cannot pass on to our children a faith and system of belief that guides our actions in the world if we don't have it ourselves. What a ministry we have—to sit with parents as they consider their responses to these questions:

- What assumptions and past experiences with the Bible need to be discarded?
- What beliefs about the Bible do you hold on to and why are they important?
- What space and time can be made for engaging the biblical story?

CHAPTER TWO

How Can We Use Children's Natural Curiosity to Help Them Read the Bible?

A story is like a labyrinth into which we step and move at whatever pace we choose; listening, wondering, questioning, reflecting, circling back and then forward as we discover new truths. We reach the centre, wait, and find meaning for ourselves in a particular time and place. As we travel back to engage in the world, we find praxis changes as well, influenced by our engagement with the story. The story becomes our own, and we live it. But the story does not remain the same, for we will enter the labyrinth again and the story will speak to us in new ways. Like ripples of water, a story is not contained. Drop a pebble into water and ripples move out and out and out. There are circles within a circle, stories within a story.

—*Susan Burt*

My sister, Rev. Cathy Hoop, was talking with Rory, a four-year-old girl and one of the "young theologians" in her congregation. They were reviewing the story of Isaiah, one of the texts for the second Sunday in Advent. My sister uses *Godly Play* with children to help them learn, remember, and connect with biblical themes and stories. With this method of storytelling (which uses wondering questions), children learn that prophets are people who listen for God's voice. My sister asked Rory if she knew a prophet. She responded, "I'm a prophet, I listen for God. And I have a friend, and she's a prophet too."

Through story and questions, Rory has already been able to connect the concept of a biblical prophet with her own experience of God.

Imagine how this simple affirmation, "I'm a prophet, I listen for God" can grow with her as she continues to read stories of God's prophets and as she continues to connect their stories to her life of faith.

Growing with God

It is a common practice for church school curriculum leader guides to include basic information about how children learn. Information about age-appropriate characteristics are included to help teachers understand what a particular group of children is able to learn and do. It is common to see information like this in church school curriculum:

Understanding the Children You Teach

Age-Appropriate Abilities with the Bible

Two and Three year olds	Four and Five year olds	Younger Elementary Grades 1-3	Older Elementary Grades 4-6
Recognizes the Bible as a special book	Interested in hearing Bible stories read from own storybook	Able to read from the Bible	Able to understand stories in their cultural context
Able to hear short Bible stories	Able to remember and help retell favorite stories	Able to learn how to use the Bible, locating stories in both testaments	Able to read on their own with a grasp of a time frame
Able to hear stories about Jesus and recognize him in pictures	Able to make simple connections between Bible stories, characters, and their life	Demonstrate a beginning ability to see how the Bible is a collection of different kinds of writing	Can use biblical tools such as dictionaries and maps
			Can articulate critical questions about text

In his research about how humans develop faith over the life course, James Fowler identified three stages of faith formation for children. From birth to age two, children are in a stage of "primal faith."[1] Essential in this stage are the child's experiences of trust and love. A child held lovingly in a parent's arms grows to know his or her world is safe, secure, full of love and care. Two year olds are able to look at and "read" board books or cloth books that have simple illustrations and minimal words. *What Is God's Name* by Rabbi Sandy Eisenberg Sasso is a great example of a book appropriate for this age group. It tells about different people who each had a different name for God. Young children (and their parents) are helped to learn that all names for God are good. At this stage of primal faith—one that is the foundation for continued growth—it is important that stories are ones that tell about positive values of love and trust so that what the child is experiencing is also reinforced with stories.

Children ages two to six are in a stage of faith that Fowler has named Intuitive-Projective. As language emerges, so also does a child's imagination, which flourishes at this age. A child at this age learns as much or more from watching what we do than from the words we speak. While she is beginning to understand symbols and the ways they represent meaning, a child at this age is not able to take the perspective of another person. Ritual and repetition characterize this stage of faith. They learn about helping others by watching a parent do a kind thing for someone else. They love to hear stories over and over and over again, to the point that they become able to "read" a loved and familiar story to their parent. Having a ritual of blessings at meals, reading Bible stories, and saying prayers at bedtime are important with this age group. And these simple repetitive activities are building blocks for a faith that grows.

As they watch what goes on around them at home and at church, they learn what it means to be part of a family. And as a child experiences the larger church family, he or she is able to know that God's love is very big, and extends beyond his or her immediate family.

Because of the richness of their imagination, children this age ask a lot of questions. Books that have questions in their titles like the ones that children ask are great ones to use in helping form their foundation of faith, such as *Where Does God Live?*, *Where Is God?*, *Does God Hear My*

Prayer?, Does God Ever Sleep?, Does God Forgive Me?, What Does God Look Like?

Kathy Bostrom has written a series of board books in the Little Blessings series on a variety of topics appropriate for young children. She answers children's questions by telling stories in rhyme, a storytelling method that children love. Her books also include help for parents by citing all the biblical texts referenced in the stories. Some of the titles are *Who Is Jesus?, Is God Always with Me?, What Is Prayer?, Why Is There a Cross?, Are Angels Real?, Who Made the World?, What Is the Bible?*

Children ages seven to twelve are in a stage of faith development that Fowler has called Mythic-Literal. School-age children are able to begin to understand story and meanings over a period of time as they move from the concrete to the ability to think abstractly. At this age, children are able to read Bible stories on their own and they become interested in details, information, action and adventure—all of which are present in the Bible. They are also able to begin to see themselves in stories and make connections between the stories they are reading and their own life.

This stage of faith development provides wonderful opportunities for supporting a child's growth in faith. As he or she gains the ability to think abstractly and are able to connect events over time, seeing perspective and how others think, these skills become evident in the questions and imagination they bring to engaging the Bible. The need for repetition that was apparent when they were younger has been replaced by a curiosity with questions about why and how and when and where.

This age is also marked by the ability of a child to make connections between the teachings of Jesus about sharing, loving others who are different from us, feeding the hungry and caring for those who are in prison—and how we are to do the same. One of the best ways a parent can help a child learn about being a Christian is to involve him or her in acts of justice, mercy, and kindness.

It is rare that this kind of information about how children develop spiritually is made available to parents. Church leaders assume a parent knows what to do. When do we help parents tune into their child's spiritual development in ways that parallel their cognitive, physical, or emotional development? T. Wyatt Watkins, pastor and author of a book about children and prayer, writes that we often underestimate "children's spiritual competencies. While spiritually, as in other realms, children are on a developmental curve, children's symbolic faith imagery, inexhaustible inquisitiveness, and characteristic candor alone qualify them for a place at the table of spiritual discourse."[2] But often that is not the case, and so the necessary environment at home that would provide the foundation for spiritual formation is sadly lacking or totally abandoned. Either children are not invited to "the table of spiritual discourse" or that table is never set.

Fears and Affirmations

There seems to be a gap between children and parents. Children bring curiosity and wonder about the Bible and parents bring fear.

Fear of the Practice of Reading the Bible

Parents, not knowing what to do, where and how to begin, or what is appropriate at a given age, often abandon any engagement with the Bible, leaving that to the church. Afraid of what they don't know, they do nothing. This fear can have many sources or roots. Some adults don't read the Bible because they simply have gotten out of the practice and don't know where or how to begin again. Afraid to admit this to anyone, they hide and never open their confirmation Bible tucked neatly away on a shelf. Others don't open it up because they have had negative experiences with the interpretation of texts and disagree with what others believe to be a correct interpretation. Adults who have gone through a divorce may have been told they are no longer welcome in the church. Gay couples who are faithful Christians leave churches where they no longer feel welcome because of how others use biblical passages to attempt to prove the limits of God's love and the church's welcome. Women who have been excluded from leadership because of texts that narrowly define the roles of women in the church seek other interpretations and wonder, like the others mentioned here, how they can continue to read the Bible. Yet they want their children to be nurtured in faith even as they may not know where or how to begin with new ways of reading and understanding the Bible, ways that don't exclude but do welcome.

THERE SEEMS TO BE A GAP BETWEEN CHILDREN AND PARENTS. CHILDREN BRING CURIOSITY AND WONDER ABOUT THE BIBLE AND PARENTS BRING FEAR.

Fear of Having Inadequate Knowledge

If their children are active participants in church school and worship, they probably have more knowledge and experience with the Bible than their parents. For many parents today their engagement with the Bible for reading or study may have stopped when they "graduated" from church after their confirmation. If parents have not been active participants in the life of the congregation or in reading the Bible on their own, then their knowledge of and engagement with biblical texts or lack of it may be something that is difficult for them to admit. Unable to face it or to return to a practice of Bible study, it becomes easier to hide and do nothing.

Fear of Immediacy

Parents may fear that they won't have an immediate answer to their child's question or won't know the right answer. This fear goes to the heart of an assumption about the Bible—that it is a primarily a book that contains right and wrong answers. When you approach the Bible from this binary position of right and wrong, or black and white, then of course you will freeze when a child asks a question you can't answer. Say, for example, you are reading along with your younger elementary-age child in the child's Bible storybook and you come to the story in Genesis 22 of Abraham and God's command to sacrifice his son, Isaac. The story is not one you would tell because you wonder about it yourself. What kind of God would ask this of someone or why would Isaac be willing to kill his son? So you hold your breath, hoping to get through it, but nope, your child pauses and looks up at you and asks you a question, the one you were afraid to verbalize. And you wonder, "What do I say? What is the right answer?" Is there a right answer? What do I believe about this story?

Affirmation of Disbelief

There are two more responses from adults that are not so much fears as they are confessions or affirmations about the Bible. There is the affirmation of "I don't believe that anymore." This is probably true of more adults than we know. And these same adults may also think that this kind of affirmation is not acceptable in the church. Believing they are the only ones who struggle with miraculous stories in the Bible or the bodily resurrection of Jesus, they are hesitant about introducing their child to the Bible.

I have some friends who wanted to join the church and have their twins baptized. They met with the church officers to discuss membership. One of the parents told the church leaders that he honestly didn't believe in the bodily resurrection of Jesus and there were other texts he was also questioning. He said that if this was a problem for them he would understand, but he still wanted to be active in this church with his family. These parents and their twins were welcomed into the life and ministry of a faithful congregation that knew and understood that questions of faith and wrestling with scripture are important parts of an adult's continuing growth as a Christian.

Affirmation of Problematic Contents

There are also parents who affirm that the Bible is full of sexism and violence. "I don't want my child growing up thinking God is a man." Some women have given up reading the Bible because of the way that women are treated within its pages, or the way women's voices are unheard, the way that male authors fail to even give women names. The fact that the authors and their perspectives are from a time and culture much different from ours is not good enough for these adults. They are concerned parents who want their children to grow up in the Christian faith with a love of God but in ways that they don't have to unlearn later.

CONCERNED PARENTS WANT THEIR CHILDREN TO GROW UP IN THE CHRISTIAN FAITH WITH A LOVE OF GOD BUT IN WAYS THAT THEY DON'T HAVE TO UNLEARN LATER.

These kinds of fears and affirmations are real for many parents. If they go unexamined, then the possibility for faith formation that happens for a child and a parent in moments of reading and reflection on Bible stories is missed. Many adults aren't musical, yet they want their child to have music lessons. The same can be said for all the other enriching activities that parents provide for their children. Jerome Berryman, an Episcopal priest and religious educator, has written about the spiritual life of children and ways that children and parents are blessed in the interaction:

> What do children need from adults and what do adults need from children for the spiritual quest? The answer is the same for both: spiritual guidance. Children require adult spiritual guidance, because they need the permission and the means to develop their spirituality. Adults require children's spiritual guidance, because by being who they are, children can refresh and re-center spiritual growth in adults. Without this mutual blessing children and adults are likely to lack the dynamic wholeness and authenticity they were created to enjoy.[3]

Perhaps our task as church leaders is to work closely with parents, helping them identify and address their fears about reading the Bible with their child. We need to provide time and space to hear their affirmations about the Bible, which are at the center of their belief system. If we teach them new ways of reading and understanding how to engage the text with their own wonder and imagination, then perhaps they can move beyond their fear. The importance of ritual with children, patterns of "faith living," is an important part of the everyday life of a family. The idea that reading a Bible story to a child could result in the adult receiving a blessing from the experience might be a new idea for some parents. "Faith teaching, in the early years, is more than anything else a process where parents and children bless each other with many experiences of trust, love and mutuality."[4]

Getting Close

Distance education is a term that graduate theological schools have used to describe an aspect of their curriculum. Living at a distance from the schools, adults with full-time jobs are able to complete degree programs by participating in intensive course work. Distance education may also describe what churches have provided for families.

Perhaps we make it too easy for parents. Perhaps we think that if our churches offer excellent Christian education programs for children, and give all our children Bibles when they enter the third grade and again at confirmation or graduation, then being at home with the Bible and developing a language of faith will be accomplished. Perhaps we haven't expected enough of parents.

Do we tell parents that raising a child in the Christian faith is not just a short hike but rather a long journey? Do we explain to them that just as families like to retell favorite stories, so too Christians do this as well? We remember who we are and whose we are as we retell, recall, and remember biblical stories. These stories of identity and formation, these hard stories of loss and recovery, these stories of promise and hope told so long ago are still our stories as we hear them in contexts much different from those of the original audience.

Do we remind parents that a congregation's program of Christian education for their child is important but not enough? Learning about God's love and Jesus's teaching through participation in a church school is a great foundation for a child but can remain distance education if parents are not involved with a close engagement with their child.

Rabbi Sandy Eisenberg Sasso is a children's author who uses story as a way into helping children grow in their understanding of who God is. She writes,

> We need to give our children stories that they can grow with. The first expression of religion is experience. We are people of faith because we had a religious experience. The closest we can get to that experience is story. Then the story is transformed into ritual and liturgy. Then comes reflection on the ritual—theology. Theology is the furthest from the experience. The closest we can get is story. We want our children to get close.[5]

Wondering as We Wander

As I mentioned in the introduction, in 1933, John Jacob Niles, a singer and folklorist, heard a young woman sing a line of a song while at a religious meeting in North Carolina. He expanded that line so it became the hymn we still sing today.

> I wonder as I wander out under the sky,
> How Jesus the savior did come for to die[6]

Niles added more verses and it became a popular hymn sung at Christmas that told of Jesus's birth. The lovely Appalachian melody is a perfect accompaniment to this song that invites the listener into a contemplative space to think about how Jesus got to the cross by starting at the beginning of his life with his birth. In this way, he expanded the telling of the story.

The quote by Susan Burt at the beginning of this chapter describes storytelling. It's similar to the experience some have of walking a labyrinth—being attentive to the pace, taking time for listening, wondering, questioning, reflecting, circling back. And then when you arrive at the center, you pause, stopping for reflection on the experience and its meaning at that particular moment.

With only a few exceptions, most Children's Bible storybooks simply tell the story, providing the biblical citation. Very few offer suggestions of how to engage the child with the story. A parent who is reading these stories to or with a child is not provided with any resources such as how to introduce the story, ways to engage the child's curiosity about the story, or how to help the child connect the story to her or his life. The goal for these storybooks seems to be simply to collect the stories that are most appropriate for a child, leaving how they are read and interpreted up to the imagination of the adult. The model seems more like a race, with a beginning and an end, rather than the experience of walking a labyrinth.

Consider another model of storytelling with a different purpose. What if the purpose of reading the story was more than a simple telling of a narrative? What if the purpose was reflection and imaginative engagement with the story and its illustrations—wondering about its meaning. If we read and tell stories with children in this way, then the stories become alive for them, inviting them to remember the stories and creating a desire to return to them again and again. Such a model enables children and parents to get close to the story, as Sasso suggests. This way of reading a biblical story invites the hearer into a dialogue.

Reading the Bible with Wonder

Many congregations have adopted a model of storytelling called *Godly Play*. It was conceived and developed by Jerome Berryman. Based on the educational principles of Maria Montessori, *Godly Play* has evolved into an extensive program of training for teachers who want to offer this in their congregation. Curricular resources that support the method are quite extensive. Basically the method involves children being invited into a space for hearing a biblical story and then responding to it.

Godly play is an interpretation of Montessori religious education, which means it is more like spiritual guidance than what is typically thought of in the church as children's education. "In Godly play, children are taught how to enter into parables, contemplative silence, sacred stories, and the liturgical action of the classical Christian language system to discover more about God, themselves, others and God's presence in the creation that surrounds and is within us."[7] This model of Christian religious education involves nurturing the spiritual development of children by teaching them language of the Christian faith, language used in the Bible and in the Christian year. It is a model that creatively integrates education, liturgy, and spiritual formation.

The story is told with sacred story boxes that include pieces made out of wood or felt. Rather than telling the story so as to transfer information and its meaning from the teacher to the child, Godly play "invites the children to make the journey of discovery for their personal theological meaning rather than memorizing concepts that others have discovered at their own arrival point."[8] At the heart of this storytelling model is the structure of the wondering questions used by the teacher to engage the children with the story after it is told. As you read the wondering questions, notice both the ways they are dealing with the biblical story and how children are invited to respond. Also notice the order of the questions and how they move a child into the story, and their response to it and connection with it.

Children are invited into sacred space by the teacher. The space provides a quiet and contemplative place to hear a story. The story is told slowly by the teacher with space for pausing as objects used in telling the story are brought out of the story box. The wondering questions at the end are also asked at a slow pace. Nothing is rushed in this method:

1. "I wonder what part of the story you like best?" This question invites their immediate response, to share what they are feeling about the story they have heard, what it evokes in them.

2. "I wonder what part of the story is the most important?" Here children are invited to think about the story and begin to make some assessment of it.

3. "I wonder where you are in the story? I wonder what part is about you?" Now the children are invited to make personal connections with the story. The conversation grows as children identify with different parts or characters. This kind of question invites them to begin to consider how this very old sacred story relates to their life today.

4. "I wonder if there is any part of the story we can leave out and still have all the story we need?" This question helps children think about the story as a whole and what is most important to the meaning.[9]

As I have watched teachers tell stories using the *Godly Play* method, I notice how children quickly adapt, how they learn to enter the circle quietly to be present to each other and to the story. I've seen how really active young children learn how to pause, and how to respond to the wondering questions that invite them both to feel and think about the story. I've seen how repetition helps them remember the different kinds of stories they will hear. For example, when hearing one of Jesus's parables they learn that parables are very old, a gift, and something that can be opened. They hear this same introduction each time a parable is told.

In addition to teaching Bible stories, *Godly Play* also helps children become familiar with the Christian calendar. Children learn to live in the rhythm of the liturgical year. So in the weeks after Easter, children are reminded that Easter is not just one Sunday, because Easter is too big to fit into only one Sunday. More time is needed in the weeks after Easter to hear more of this sacred story.

Observing children and teachers participating in the approach to telling Bible stories used in the *Godly Play* resources, it quickly becomes apparent that the storytelling process has these values: quiet contemplation, a slow pace of storytelling that uses visual symbols to help tell the story, and wondering questions for children that encourage and invite their response. The approach also helps them connect stories with seasons of the church year. I have often wondered how this model could be adapted so as to be made available for a parent to use at home with a child. And this led me to think about building on the *Godly Play* wondering model of questions and how this model can be used by parents at home.

A Wondering Model of Questions

One of the steps in the *Godly Play* model of storytelling that really works well with children is that of inviting them into the space, helping them to learn how to be quiet and ready to hear the story. Making a commitment to reading the Bible with a child as a way to close the day provides a ritual that can become important both for the parent and the child. All it requires is time that is not rushed and a good Bible storybook.

MAKING A COMMITMENT TO READING THE BIBLE WITH A CHILD AS A WAY TO CLOSE THE DAY PROVIDES A RITUAL THAT CAN BECOME IMPORTANT BOTH FOR THE PARENT AND THE CHILD.

Enter

Find that place where you will read together. It may be a comfortable chair or it may be the child's bedroom, with you sitting next the child. As you begin to help a child make the transition from play time or a bath to this special time, questions like these can help with the transition:

- How was your day today?
- Was there something that made you really laugh?
- Was there something that made you sad?

Or you could use a variation of the *Examen*, an ancient spiritual practice of examining the day before going to sleep. The *Examen* asks you to be aware of God's presence as you review the day.

- Where did you see God's love today?
- Where did you give or receive God's love? For what are you most grateful?
- For what are you least grateful?

Entering the space together provides a time of unwinding, a settling down for both parent and child. Parents need this moment as much as their child. So entering this space with some deep breaths and awareness of the places where you have been this day is a good place for a parent to begin. It can be a place for dialogue as children and a parent(s) share their stories of the day—sads and glads, stories that can be filled with humor and pathos. In this sharing together, children and adults learn the discipline of spiritual practices together.

Hear

Reading the story together can be done several ways. You can simply follow in order the stories that are included in the storybook you are using. You could be familiar with the stories that are being used in your child's church school class and be sure to read that one in the week preceding and following the Sunday it is used.

Young children love repetition, so as this practice continues over time, a child may request to hear a story repeated. The more they hear a story, obviously the more familiar they are with it and become able to tell it themselves. Another way to tell the story is to show a video of it on a tablet or computer. This requires some advance work of locating, previewing, and evaluating what is available. For example, *YouTube* has the story of Jesus blessing the children, told by Desmond Tutu from the Gospel of Mark. It is the same story told in his book, *Children of God Storybook Bible. The Deep Blue Kids Bible* has an app that includes many of the features that are included in this version of the *Common English Bible* for children.

Pause

This may not be the easiest or most natural step, but when tried, it may become an important part of this practice of wondering. Pausing means we take a few seconds, maybe a minute, just to sit with the story in silence. Of course, this is not so easy with young children. But the practice can grow with them. With a three year old, you could count to ten silently with fingers and when you have counted all ten, then it's time to move to wondering questions.

Wonder

This part of the model invites the child to explore the story. It's helpful if a parent has read the story ahead of time but this is not required. What is important for a parent to remember is not to be fearful of the child's questions. If she or he asks a question requiring a specific answer, it's always OK to respond, "That's a great question, why don't we try to find an answer for it together?"

Simpler questions are best with younger children; some questions that can be used to help a child engage and reflect on the story are these:

1. Who is in the story and what happens to them?

This is a great question for all ages, especially young children. With this basic question, children are introduced to a tool of literary analysis of text that seeks to identify in each story the characters, the setting, and the plot. Older children are, of course, able to identify the plot more easily than younger children. As they respond to the question about who is in the story, other questions you could use are: Why questions (*Why do you think Jonah ran away?*) and/or What if questions (*What if Jonah had said yes to God rather than no?*).

2. What do you think this story is about?

If the story is one that Jesus told, you could ask, "Why do you think Jesus told this story?" This is a good open-ended question because it invites the hearer to respond with his or her own interpretation. Just imagine how a child's answer to this question could change as he or she grows older.

3. What kind of story is this?

This question is more appropriate for older children who are reading on their own and know about different kinds of writing. For example, the story of Miriam, Esther, Abraham, or Moses would be an example of history. A psalm would be an example of poetry or song. This is also an example of how stories from the Bible can grow with the child, that there is more to explore, more to learn. This helps a child want to return to a familiar story.

4. How is this story different from the time and place in which we live?

This question works best for older children. It invites them to wonder about the time and culture and the original audience for which the story was written. This kind of thinking encourages a child to think about the text from a historical point of view, a kind of biblical analysis that scholars have been using for a long time. It also provides a beginning step in cultural analysis, understanding the story and its meaning for the reader who hears it in a very different time and place. Inviting a child to notice the artwork accompanying the story is a good way to engage this question, too.

5. Why do you think this story is important?

This kind of question asks children for their own analysis of the story. With younger children you could ask, "Do you like this story? Why or why not?"

6. How do you connect with the story or what does this story have to do with your life? Or, When would be a good time to remember this story?

This kind of question helps children affirm the ways they connect their life with this very old story. It also helps them see how a story written a very long time ago still has meaning today.

The movement of the questions is designed so as to help a child recall and remember the facts and actions of the story. Then they are encouraged to step back and reflect on the meaning of the story and the ways they connect with it. Using a wondering model of reflection on a biblical story helps children trust their own voices, giving them an experience of being comfortable with asking questions of the story and trusting first steps in forming their own interpretive responses.

Bless

As you end this practice of reading the Bible together, select one or more of the following that work for you:

- Affirm some of the things you have heard the child say about the story.
- Recall some of the good things or bad things mentioned by the child at the beginning and use them in a simple prayer of thanks or a prayer for help.
- Invite the child to pray. This could help her or him learn how to use different kinds of prayers. With adults we talk about prayers of Adoration, Confession, Thanksgiving and Supplication (ACTS). We can teach children similar kinds of prayers of "Thanks, Gimme, Wow, and Oops."[10] Learning to say thanks to God, making prayer requests, expressing awe, sadness or lament, and confessing are all important foundations for spiritual life. An additional kind of prayer important to teach children is prayer of intercession or "God, please remember." This is a great way to invite children to name the people and places they want to remember in prayer.

Principles of a Wondering Model of Reading Biblical Stories with Children

A simple approach to engaging children with Bible story through five steps (Enter, Hear, Pause, Wonder, Bless) has been offered. Behind this model are four important principles that support a child's engagement of the biblical story with wonder and imagination. These principles support the model. They are like the footnotes at the bottom of the page or the small print in the notes of a study Bible. They provide the rationale for this model, connecting how we tell Bible stories, while also keeping in mind who the hearers are, appropriate learning methods, and good biblical scholarship.

A Wondering Model Invites Children to Have a Conversation with the Biblical Story

The stories that are provided for children to hear and read are rich, full of places for engagement. They tell about God's relationship with creation and people who lived in a time and culture so very different from our own. These kinds of stories invite children to engage them. When we invite children to hear such stories, we are also inviting and supporting their interpretations. This kind of conversation with a biblical text can be described as polyphonic because a dialogue takes place between the hearer and the text. A biblical story is monologic when it doesn't invite the response of the child. It is monologic when it reduces a story or attempts to tame the text to make it simpler.

CONVERSATION WITH A BIBLICAL TEXT CAN BE DESCRIBED AS POLYPHONIC BECAUSE A DIALOGUE TAKES PLACE BETWEEN THE HEARER AND THE TEXT.

In describing textual reading that is polyphonic, Mark Roncace reminds us about the value of literature in helping us understand others. He writes,

> Polyphonic literature...serve[s] as a model of conversation, showing us how other voices can and should be heard.... The diversity of the Bible can serve as a wonderful resource not only for exploring with children the complexities of the world around them but also for preparing them to plumb the depths of the spiritual and religious life in the Jewish and Christian traditions.[11]

Consider a very familiar story included in most Bible storybooks and how it might enable conversations about difference and diversity. The translator of Genesis in the *Common English Bible* has given a new title to the very familiar story of the Tower of Babel in Genesis 11:1-9, "Origin of Languages and Cultures." When you read Genesis 11:1-9 in *The Deep Blue Kids Bible*, it is important to notice the difference in the way this story has been translated. For centuries this story has been interpreted as a story about a tower that people were building out of pride. The interpretation continues that they were so full of pride and arrogance that they believed they could build a tower that would reach heaven. When God saw what they were doing, God knew they would succeed, and God punished them by giving them different languages to speak, and so not being able to understand each other, they were dispersed from Shinar. In this traditional interpretation, diversity of language and culture is the result of punishment. This story is told and interpreted this way in most children's Bible storybooks. The illustration of the tower is always the central picture of the story.

The *Common English Bible* translation included in *The Deep Blue Kids Bible* translates the story differently. Hearing the difference in the translation requires simply reading and hearing the story without the overlay of previous interpretations of pride and punishment. When those are removed a new theme emerges. The people of Shinar knew each other and liked living together. They were so happy with their homogeneity that they decided to build a city and a tower. In seeing what they were doing and realizing that they would continue to enjoy being together, all alike, God decided to mix them up and send them out so they would learn to live with those who are different from themselves. Theodore Hiebert, the translator of Genesis in the *Common English Bible*, provides an interpretation of his new translation of the Hebrew. "So God put God's own plan into effect, introducing the cultural diversity and difference that make the world the complex, rich, and sometimes challenging place it actually is. Whereas the human plan for community aimed at sameness, God's plan for community aimed at distinctiveness, complexity, and multiformity."[12]

Children can be invited to wonder about this story when they are invited to think about it with questions such as:

- Why do you think they liked living together?
- They really enjoyed living with people who were just like themselves. Who is someone you know who is really different from you? How is he or she different? What do you like or enjoy about this person?

- What's something you have learned from someone who is not exactly like you?

A Wondering Model Invites the Child to Hear or Read the Story with Question Marks, not Periods[13]

Important here are the ways that children are able to engage the complexities of the story. Rather than simplifying the narrative, a wondering model invites children into the story in ways that will make them want to return to it again. When a story is told so as to lead a child to a simple moral truth, it is simplified, interpreted for the child, rather than told for engagement with questions that invite his or her curiosity and questions. Inviting children into conversation with the story supports the abilities that they are learning in school. Reading the Bible in this way they learn how to "engage, evaluate, and interact with different voices in the text—that is, they learn to think critically and to be spiritually and ethically sensitive human beings."[14]

The story of Zacchaeus told in Luke 19 is a most familiar story, included in every children's Bible storybook. *Candle Read and Share* gives it the title of "A Very Short Man." It's told simply on two pages and focuses on Zaccheus wanting to see Jesus and then Jesus inviting himself to Zaccheus's home. The text box question invites the children to wonder what it would be like if Jesus came to *their* house: "What would you do if Jesus came to see you?"[15]

Desmond Tutu's *Children of God Storybook Bible* adds more information about Zacchaeus and his work as a tax collector and how he became rich because he cheated people. It includes dialogue from the people who had lost their money. The scene in Zacchaeus's home concludes with Zacchaeus promising to return the money he had taken and Jesus's comment, "Today you have become a new man. Now you can truly stand tall."[16] The concluding prayer is one asking for help with being fair and honest.

AS CHILDREN GROW IN THEIR ABILITIES TO TAKE THE PERSPECTIVE OF OTHERS, THIS STORY GROWS WITH THEM.

This is a story that grows with a child and one that invites reading with question marks. As they age, children will have questions about why people didn't like Zaccheus. They will surely be able to relate to the concept of cheating and what that does to the person who cheats and to those who are cheated. As children grow in their ability to take the perspective of others, this story grows with them.

A Wondering Model Helps Children Get It Right the First Time so They Don't Have to Unlearn Things Later

This idea was first expressed by a student in seminary who was exasperated with the ways children are taught biblical stories. He wondered out loud why it was only in seminary that he learned about the two stories of creation in Genesis, two stories from the perspective of two authors. He immediately became convinced of the importance of helping children read the Bible so they don't have to unlearn things later.[17] When stories are told accurately with good biblical scholarship, then children's knowledge and experiences with the Bible will continue to grow.

Children in elementary grades are learning literary skills of analysis and different kinds of writing. What a great way to invite their literary skills to be used in reading the two stories of Genesis told in chapters 1 and 2. This is an example of helping children read a story in ways they don't have to unlearn later. The birth stories of Jesus in Matthew and Luke are another example of how children can learn that two different authors told the same story.

A Wondering Model Invites a Child and a Parent to Reflect on the Text and Illustrations of Stories in the Bible

Making time for reading Bible stories with children requires intention and commitment. It means a parent or other adult pauses from other things. It requires turning off the noise of phones and messaging and emails and turning attention toward precious time sitting with a child and a timeless story. It's not a race to get through but a spiritual practice for both child and adult. It introduces a child to the stories of faith where they begin to learn about God's love as it is told through the stories of people in the Bible. Illustrations that accompany the story contribute to a child's imaginative engagement with the story.

I grew up reading a story Bible that included many stories, some with illustrations. It stayed on the table by my bed and was a favorite choice for reading before bed. One story became my favorite, Hannah and her prayer to Jesus for a child, and then the story of her son, Samuel, whom she sent to live with the priest Eli. I loved hearing a woman's story. The story of God calling Samuel in the middle of the night opened up my own curiosity about the mystery of God.

PAUSING WITH CHILDREN TO READ AND TO WONDER ABOUT MEANINGS IN WORDS AND IN ILLUSTRATIONS OF BIBLE STORIES IS A SPIRITUAL PRACTICE.

The story of the temptation of Jesus told in Matthew 4, and Mark 1 is a great example of how illustrations invite children to wonder about the story. In their illustrations, both the *Augsburg Story Bible* and *Candle Read and Share* depict the devil as a shadowy-type of person painted in very close to Jesus. The picture invites children to think about the story in relation to themselves. Who or what has tempted them to do something wrong or not good? In *Lion Read and Know*, the devil is pictured as a snake. *Shine On: A Story Bible* pictures a very contemplative Jesus sitting on a rock, holding a stone.

Pausing with children to read and to wonder about the meanings in words and illustrations of Bible stories is a spiritual practice. All it requires is a commitment to space and time to imagine together about how we hear and respond to these timeless stories.

Cautions about a Wondering Model

This model invites and expects an approach to biblical texts that is honest and curious, open to inquiry and interpretation. Its focus and intent is on how a child is first introduced to biblical story in a way that encourages their questions, curiosities, and all of their imagination. It supports a child's spiritual development as they grow with a story, in understanding its meaning and the possible connections it has for their life. It is a model of engaging the biblical text that values open-ended responses rather than right or wrong answers. As such it seeks to empower children and the adults who read with them with the ability to see the connections between these old stories and how we see God revealed in them.

This model invites the reader and hearer beyond a reading of the Bible that only provides a binary understanding of good and bad. Timothy Beal has wrestled with this observation and has written:

> One major effect of the Bible as generated in and by children's Bibles is its contribution to the cultural production of Christian faith as black-and-white certainty and religiosity as right-and-wrong morality. The Bible, as cultural icon of this supposedly childlike faith, is the book of books, the authoritative, univocal, comprehensive, final, graspable, and readable word of God. God publishes it to answer questions about the meaning and purpose of life, putting them to rest in the name of its divine author. It is the manual and guidebook for finding happiness with God in this world and salvation in the next.[18]

Parents who were raised with this kind of certainty, who were taught to believe in the Bible as the literal word of God, either continue to teach that to their children or begin to wonder if there is another way to approach the Bible and at the same time examine their own beliefs. Beal wonders "what potentials are there for children's Bibles to open spaces in which a kind of deconstruction of that binary world can be hosted."[19]

He suggests that using Marshall McLuhan's categories of "hot" and "cold" media can be applied to biblical stories. A story that is "hot" is one that has a lot of definition, filled with information, thus expecting lower participation from the hearer. Beal contrasts this with a story that is "cool," less defined, revealing more gaps in the narrative and thereby inviting increased participation and response from the reader: "With very few exceptions, children's Bibles are *hottings-up of the biblical text*, revising and filling in both literary and visual data in such a way as to remove ambiguities, tensions, and gaps that otherwise leave biblical texts cool and invite participation from their young audiences."[20]

A STORY THAT IS "HOT" IS ONE THAT HAS A LOT OF DEFINITION. A STORY THAT IS "COOL" IS LESS DEFINED, REVEALING MORE GAPS IN THE STORY AND THEREBY INVITING INCREASED PARTICIPATION AND RESPONSE FROM THE READER.

This is the result when a text is read so as to produce a moral for the child. The story of the binding of Isaac in Genesis and the parables of Jesus are two good examples of "cool" texts that leave space for wrestling and connection. The story of Jesus in the temple as a child can be an example of a "hot" text when with words and visual images it is reduced to a moral lesson about obedience to parents.

Getting Close to the Bible with Children

When a parent brings the Bible close to a child, the parent also comes close. How we help children learn a faith vocabulary that connects biblical stories with living a life of faith requires commitment to opening space in busy lives. Such a space for hearing and wondering about stories in the Bible values and invites parent and child to hear the stories in new ways, as Burt suggests, because "the story does not remain the same." Opening space, hearing and reading the Bible again with new questions and wonderings, is an opportunity for relationship: parent and child, parent and child and the Bible, parent and child and living a life of faith.

In his introduction to his book of Bible stories, Rabbi Marc Gellman writes, "The Bible is kind of like a pair of glasses though which I look at the world. I see our stories in its stories. I see all of us in all of them, and most of all I see God there and I see God here.... So don't lose your questions about stories in the Bible. They are like the cherry inside the chocolate. They are the reason God made Moses schlep up to the top of Mount Sinai to get all this for us."[21]

How we help parents move beyond their fears so they are free to support their child's questions, wonderings, and curiosities about the Bible is so important. When parents are able to make the space and take the time to read the Bible with children, all are blessed. In giving of themselves in this way to a child, they do indeed provide their child with a way to view the world through the lens of faith.

CHAPTER THREE

What Bibles and Bible Storybooks Do We Read with Children?

Stories give us the sources of our identity, our origins, our nature, our destiny as persons and as a people. Stories give us models of character, examples to follow, and examples to avoid. Stories give us indications of the nature and the disposition of God. They show us God's suffering and pain and God's compassion. Stories give us indications of the way life is and of the disciplines that are required to live it well, with courage and resourcefulness.

—James Fowler

Perhaps you have heard these questions asked or you may have asked them yourself:

- I want to give a Bible storybook to my grandchild. Which one do I give?
- My friend's daughter is being baptized, and I want to give them a good Bible storybook. What do you recommend?
- Our church gives a Bible or Bible storybook on three occasions—at baptism, third grade, and confirmation. We want a good translation and we want one that the children will actually use and be able to understand. What do you recommend?
- We like to have children's Bibles or storybooks available in the church school classrooms. Which ones are most appropriate

for preschoolers and younger and older elementary-age children?

- It's hard to know what Bible storybook to select for my child. I'm overwhelmed when I look at all the titles that are available. What are some criteria I should consider when shopping for one? Do I make a decision based on which stories are included? How important is the translation or the way the story is told?

- Artwork in children's Bible storybooks is important to me. I really want the people to look like they are from the Middle East. What do you recommend?

I have a small but growing collection of children's Bible storybooks. They share some things in common, but for the most part it's their differences that are more obvious. Some are recent publications and some are over ten years old. All share a common purpose: to help children become familiar with stories from the Old and New Testaments.

Try typing in "Children's Bible storybooks" on a bookstore website and watch the dizzying array appear, with titles such as: *Lift the Flap Bible, Beginners Bible, God's Little Princess Devotional Bible.* There are stories for bedtime, stories for babies, stories to read aloud, stories for day-by-day, and the list goes on for over one hundred pages. And they come in varieties of shapes and sizes. Perhaps that is where grandparents are finding the storybooks that they give to their grandchildren in hopes they will grow up knowing familiar and beloved Bible stories.

In making decisions about which storybooks to review and evaluate for this chapter, I, too, have been ordering them online and finding an interesting selection available as used books. What is fascinating is to open a used children's Bible and read the inscription, "For Megan from Nana and Pop, Christmas 2010." I had an immediate reaction. This inscription was written on the book *Candle Read and Share*, which is a good storybook for young children. I thought how sad, that this storybook may have never been opened. It is in pristine condition so it must have been resold immediately before it could be used. I wondered about the grandparents who gave the storybook, hoping their son or daughter would raise their grandchild in the life of the Christian faith. I wondered about the parents of Nana and Pop's grandchild and what their intentions were, if any, about reading Bible stories and helping their child find their way in the world with the eyes of faith.

A copy of *Jesus Calling, Bible Storybook* by Sarah Young was inscribed "For Christopher from Grandpa and Grandma, Christmas, 2014." Just like the previous book, this was one sold as used but appears to be in perfect condition. I had a different reaction, wondering about why this book had been discarded and ended up being sold by a used book vendor. I imagined that a parent did want to raise her child in the life of the Christian faith and wanted him to learn Bible stories. But she didn't want him to learn them in the way they are presented in this book. In this book of beautifully illustrated stories, no Old Testament narrative is allowed to stand alone as a treasured story of how God loved God's people. Each story is not only connected to Jesus but includes additional verses that the author has selected to support the theme of the story. Hopefully this wise parent knew this kind of storytelling would be confusing to a child and so she decided to let this book go. Or maybe she also wanted her child to grow up with many images for God, and so she wanted a storybook that did not call God *He*. I wonder if this parent would have talked with her own parents about why the storybook was not appropriate and helped them find one that was a better choice.

Storybooks and Children's Bibles— What's the Difference?

So where and how do you begin to select a Bible or storybook to use at home or at church? Initially it's important to look at the title. The majority of Bibles for children include one of these words in the title: story Bible, storybook Bible, children's Bible, read and share, or read and know.

When you see the word *story* or *storybook*, then you know that you are getting a collection of stories from the Bible, selected by the author or editor. *Bible storybook* is the most appropriate title since the focus is on a storytelling version of the Bible. Some Bible storybooks will add additional words that provide a clue about their hope for the reader such as "read and know" or "read and share." Titles such as *Children's Bible* or *Kids' Bible* are used when there is a whole Bible for the child to read, one that includes the entire Bible, not selected Bible stories.

Bible storybooks share the following things in common: *The content is a collection of stories retold from the Bible.* This content is described in various ways and provides an angle of vision about the approach to biblical interpretation that is at work. Several of the Bible storybooks reviewed here make clear a thematic or theological approach to scripture.

In *The Jesus Storybook Bible: Every Story Whispers His Name*, the introduction provides a clear distinction about what the Bible is and states that though some consider it to be a book of rules or a book about heroes, in fact it is a story, "one Big Story. The Story of how God loves his children and comes to rescue them. It takes the whole Bible to tell this Story. And at the center of the Story, there is a baby. Every Story in the Bible whispers his name."[1] Twenty-one Old Testament and twenty-three New Testament stories are included in this Bible storybook.

Shine On, a storybook published by the Mennonites, includes this orienting theme in the introduction: "God's light: breaking through in creation, coming into the world through Jesus, and shining today in our lives. Jesus said, 'You are the light of the world.' This thread of light, woven through the Bible, is now passed on to you through engaging stories and colorful images demonstrating the rich witness of the people of God."[2]

The *International Children's Story Bible*'s orienting theme is how God loves every person, "regardless of race, nationality or culture.... As you read the Bible stories to your child, discuss with them how people in other countries view God and how much He loves each one of us."[3]

The author of the retold stories in *The Bible for Children* writes in the introduction about how the themes that we read in the Bible are timeless. He provides a realistic caution that the stories in the Bible are about real people who struggle and who sometimes fail. "This is a love story: the moving tale of God's love for the world in all its wonder and all its brokenness. It is full of beauty and hope, but it is also very realistic about people and the consequences of their actions."[4]

It is also possible to identify a theological theme or orientation to stories as you examine individual stories told in Bible storybooks. For example, in the story of Jonah and the Big Fish in *Five-Minute Bible Stories* by Lois Rock, the story ends with God's conversation with Jonah who is so upset about the plant dying. God says to Jonah, "Well, if you can care about a plant, I can care about Nineveh. I love Nineveh. I love its people, I love the children, and I love the animals. That's the kind of God I am."[5] In a simple declarative sentence, Rock helps children get a glimpse of the nature of God.

In identifying an organizing theme—whispers of Jesus's name, light of God, love of God for all—the editors hope that children will be able to read individual stories and begin to see how the stories connect with each other and with the theme. Whether or not this connection is made depends upon how intentional the storybook is in helping readers to move beyond individual stories in the Bible.

The Content of Story Bibles Has Remarkable Consistency in Terms of What Is Included and What Is Omitted

If you read the introduction and scan the contents, the approach that is taken for choice of stories becomes clear. Most simply divide the stories into the Old and New Testament.

Ellen Frankel is the author of the *JPS* (Jewish Publication Society) *Illustrated Children's Bible*. She writes in the introduction that her selection of the fifty-three stories was guided by her "sense of what makes a good story for children, but a few were included because they are pivotal to an understanding of the Jewish national story."[6] She includes a very helpful article, "Writing a Jewish Children's Bible: An Author's Notebook" at the end, where she states that her "chief aim in writing this book has been to introduce American children to the language and rhythms of the Hebrew Bible."[7] How different this approach is from the one that simply wants to tell the story. Frankel hopes that in reading stories she has written, children will become attentive to the culture out of which the stories have been written.

Two storybooks provide a particular approach to organizing the content. *A People Listen for God* provides stories from the "Old Covenant" (their term) under these headings: *Roots of a People, Birth of a People, People Want a King, People of Israel in Exile, Re-establishment of a People.* Stories in the New Covenant or New Testament are included with these headings: *Jesus of Nazareth—Proclamation of the Kingdom, Jesus of Nazareth—Death and Resurrection, Apostles Proclaim Jesus.*

The Pilgrim Book of Bible Stories, written for older children (nine to twelve years), indicates in the introduction that it seeks to balance the stories with the Bible, "so weight is given to the laws of Leviticus, the Song of Solomon, and many passages usually ignored. Wisdom literature, prophecy, vision and parable are given as much space as historical adventure."[8] The stories that are included are organized into these categories: Instruction, history, wisdom, song, and prophets comprise the stories from the Old Testament. And Gospels, journeys, letters and Revelation are the ways that stories from the New Testament are grouped.

The majority of storybooks reviewed here do not provide a rationale for selection of the content. There seems to be some implicit understanding about what stories are appropriate for children. So, for example, all will include the story of Jonah because the image of the big fish is so vivid for young readers. Some tell the whole story of Jonah and others will omit the ending, leaving off Jonah's pouting under the shrub and the final conversation with God. Few storybooks include the book of Job or prophets like Isaiah, Jeremiah, Micah, Amos, and Hosea.

The content of New Testament storybooks is remarkably similar. Though there is some variation about which persons Jesus meets (Mary and Martha are always included while the Samaritan woman Jesus met at the well is only occasionally included) and which healing and miracle stories are told, the majority of the stories focus on the Gospels. All include a few stories of the early church in Acts and some of the female and male leaders. Very few include any mention of the Epistles. Most jump from the stories of the early church to the book of Revelation.

KEEP IN MIND WHICH TEXTS SIMPLY PROVIDE GOOD STORIES FOR CHILDREN AND WHICH ONES ARE IMPORTANT IN HELPING A CHILD CLAIM HER OR HIS IDENTITY AS ONE OF GOD'S OWN.

Frankel's criteria for story selection is useful as you read through a Bible storybook. Keep in mind which texts simply provide good stories for children and which ones are important in helping a child claim her or his identity as one of God's own. Which stories are essential for understanding the rhythm of the one story of God's love told across both testaments and which ones provide a language of faith, essential for a child's growing vocabulary of theological language?

The stories are written in various styles. This information is available either in the front of the book with the publishing information or in an introduction to the book. For example, *The Crossroad Children's Bible* describes the content as a "retelling in simplified language of the stories from the Old and New Testaments."[9] The *Spark Story Bible* tells the reader that the stories that have been included have been "retold." *The Pilgrim Book of Bible Stories* indicates on the cover page that the stories have been "retold in a fresh and lively way for today's children."[10]

Sometimes the storybook will provide information about the translation upon which the retold stories are based. The *Candle Read and Share Bible* includes stories that have been retold based on *The Holy Bible: International Children's Bible.* Some, like *The Jesus Storybook Bible: Every Story Whispers His Name*, includes rewritten Bible stories with the note that quotations from the Bible are taken from *The Holy Bible, New International Version. The Pilgrim Book of Bible Stories* and *Shine On: A Story Bible* both include scripture from the New Revised Standard Version of the Bible.

Ralph Milton, author of *The Family Story Bible* and *The Lectionary Story Bible: Volumes A, B, C,* provides the clearest statement about how the stories are written in his comment for adults who will read the stories with children. He is clear that he brings imagination to the stories: "Where the terse biblical text offers little detail, I add my own. Where names are missing, I invent them. Where connecting narrative is absent, I supply it. Then I add my own dash of drama and suspense and fun. Sometimes, almost the whole story comes from my imagination and almost none of it from the Bible. If that bothers you, maybe you need to find another book."[11]

Storybooks Often Provide a Table of Contents Where They List the Stories (by Title and/or Citation)

Shine On Story Bible, *Pilgrim Book of Bible Stories*, and *Candle Read and Share Bible* offer a descriptive title and text citation. The *Jesus Storybook Bible* and *The Lion Read and Know Bible* all provide imaginative titles for the Bible stories. When the table of contents provides only a story title, the text citation is included with the story.

Artwork to Illustrate the Stories Is Included

The form of artwork found in Bible storybooks includes three styles: Child-friendly contemporary, drawings, and storybooks that include a mix of both. In addition some storybooks will use one artist for all illustrations (*Pilgrim Book of Bible Stories*) and some will include different artists with different styles of illustrations (*Children of God Storybook Bible* by Desmond Tutu and *Shine On: A Story Bible*). *The Pilgrim Book of Bible Stories* hired an Israeli artist, many of whose pictures were drawn in the places she was illustrating.

The *International Children's Story Bible* theme of God's love for all people is made explicit in the choice to invite children from around the world to provide the illustrations. They do this out of the concern that the illustrations often included in children's Bible storybooks have people who don't look at all different from us.

Bibles for children that include the whole Bible are fewer in number. The best example is *The Deep Blue Kids Bible* which offers the newest translation of the Bible, the *Common English Bible*, with a variety of side-bar notes and helps for children including an introduction to each book of the Bible.

Criteria for Selection

The number and variety of Bible storybooks available for purchase can only add to the confusion about how to make a selection. It's easy to be drawn to the catchy titles or covers as you think about what will be attractive or interesting to a child. Another perspective asks:

- What Bible storybook will help my child become familiar with some of the important stories?
- What Bible storybook will help my child begin to wonder about God and Jesus and the Spirit and want to know more?
- What kinds of stories and illustrations will enable my child to wonder about God's place in his or her life?
- Which one provides help for my child in understanding the meaning of the text?

In a recent article in *The Christian Century*, Sarah Hinlicky Wilson introduced her critique of children's Bibles. She dares to suggest that the Bible is really not a book that is appropriate for children to read,

> neither in its unsavory parts—murders, rapes, genocides, betrayals, mauling by wild animals, curses, divine retribution and apocalyptic horrors—nor in many of its neutral or even uplifting parts, including statutes and ordinances, proverbs, genealogies, geographies, prophecies, censuses, and pretty much all of the epistles. It's no surprise that most of these sections get dropped from children's versions altogether, though at some point we may begin to wonder with what justification they still call themselves Bibles. Scripture is definitely something to ease the little ones into, not drop them in cold. So what's the best way to go about it?[12]

Wilson is correct in saying that a large amount of the more difficult parts of the Bible, are not included in children's Bible storybooks. None of the twelve storybooks reviewed here included anything from Leviticus or a majority of the minor prophets. Wisdom literature was rarely included, and few included anything from the prophets other than one story from Amos, Hosea, Isaiah, or Micah. Her suggestion that the Bible is a book that children need help easing into is worth considering.

In contrast to Wilson's observation about the challenges present in reading the Bible with children, Melanie Dennis Unrau raises the question "Where are the girls in the Children's Bibles?" In her review and critique of children's Bible storybooks, she uses five criteria—"the five P's of a feminist picture Bible":

- Inclusive language for God is used. God is not referenced with a gender pronoun.
- Illustrations used with Bible stories include people of color. People in stories from the Old and New Testament look like they live in the Middle East.
- As stories are retold, there is an attempt to offer a critique of power. Issues of sexism, racism, or power are indicated in the way the story is told.[13]
- The selection of stories includes women whose voice is heard or whose actions are revealed.
- At least half of the illustrations that are in the storybook include pictures of women or girls.[14]

Using these criteria, she evaluates Bible Storybooks (collections of Bible stories) and individual Bible stories to evaluate them as those which can't be redeemed, those are a bit better, some that are redeemable with a bit of work, and those that she recommends.

Both of these authors then reviewed and critiqued a small selection of children's Bibles. I was surprised by some of the choices they made and by what books were not included in their list. Using the approach of Wilson and some of the critieria of Unrau, I would like to recommend the following Bibles and Bible storybooks that I think are excellent choices both for kids and parents and other family members who want to read the Bible with children so that this practice is embedded in their life of growing in the Christian faith.

Consider these criteria when selecting a Bible storybook:

1. Content

   - Which books/stories are included/omitted? Why?
   - How many Old Testament and New Testament stories are present?
   - How is the story told? Are text references included? Does it invite wonder? Does it fill in gaps in the story? Does it conflate or harmonize texts? (For example, does it tell the birth story of Jesus putting together the stories from Matthew and Luke rather than telling the story with the differences from the two Gospels?)
   - What translation of the Bible is the story based on?
   - Are the stories from the Old Testament allowed to stand on their own without being connected to stories of Jesus?
   - Is inclusive language for God used?

2. Organization, ease of use for parents and children, resources, index

   - Is there an introduction for parents or children?
   - Is the biblical citation given for the stories?
   - Is there any kind of introduction to the two testaments and to the different kinds of writing in each?
   - What additional resources, if any, does this Bible storybook have?
   - Is there an index of stories or table of contents?

3. Layout and appropriateness for reader—what helps the child understand and interpret the story for their lives? Are there questions that invite the child to engage the story?

4. Art

   - What kind of art is used to illustrate the stories—realistic, contemporary, child friendly?
   - In what ways do the illustrations contribute to the story?

Easing Children into the Bible

Beginning with young children, criteria that are important in selecting a storybook Bible to read to and with preschool children ages two to five include these:

- Content and length of story—how much of the story is told? In its simplification or rewriting of the story, is the main point of the story still there? The story needs to be no more than two to three paragraphs.
- Illustrations—what kind of illustrations are included (characters, drawings)? Do they invite the child into the story?
- Support for parents—are any suggestions available to parents?

The Children's Everyday Bible

This title (New York: DK Publishing, 2001) includes one story for every day of the year, 193 from the Old Testament and 172 from the New Testament. They are offered in sequence, with the story of creation from Genesis 1 offered on January 1. The stories are short, only one paragraph, and are well illustrated. For young children, reading one story a day would work. Four and five year olds might want an additional story. This book could have been helped by including a wondering question for reflection with the children.

The International Children's Story Bible

A story Bible by Mary Hollingsworth (Thomas Nelson, 1993), this book selects 105 stories that represent diversity in the kinds of writing found in the Bible: history, wisdom literature, Gospels, and letters. Stories are chosen for their accessibility to younger children. Each story is one page with an accompanying illustration drawn by a child. In the letter to parents at the beginning, the publisher reminds the reader of "God's love for every person, regardless of race, nationality or culture. Yet, we often portray God's Word to our children through illustrations of people who look just like ourselves."[15] Though this book is older, it is still available from used booksellers.

Children of God Storybook Bible

This book (Grand Rapids: Zonderkidz, 2010) by Archbishop Desmond Tutu shares a similar commitment to helping children begin to read the Bible from a multicultural perspective. The fifty-six stories are chosen to show the ways that God works through history and how God wants all people to love each other. In their commitment to designing a global children's Bible, the stories are illustrated by artists from around the world. Each story is on two pages and ends with a prayer. There are twenty-four stories from the Old Testament and thirty-one from the New Testament. All but five of the New Testament stories focus on the Gospels. The deluxe edition includes a CD with Tutu reading the stories. The boxed set with the CD makes a lovely gift for a family at a birth, adoption, or baptism of a child.

Candle Read and Share Bible

This book (United Kingdom: Thomas Nelson, 2007) includes 208 "bite-size Stories" as they are described in the letter to the parents at the beginning. The stories include some books that are often omitted from children's Bible storybooks: Esther, Job, Ecclesiastes, and Isaiah. With longer texts from the Old Testament, like Noah for example, the story is divided into five short segments. Each story includes the biblical citation and a comment or a question for the child to consider. The illustrations are bright and colorfully drawn in a character (cartoon style) that works well with young children.

The Family Story Bible and *The Lectionary Story Bible*

The Family Story Bible (Louisville: Westminster John Knox Press, 1996) includes fifty-eight stories from the Old Testament and sixty-seven from the New Testament. It is a good choice for the kindergarten-age child who enjoys hearing stories and is learning basic reading skills. As young children improve with their reading skills, *The Family Story Bible* and *The Lectionary Story Bible* can become important storybooks for introductions to many treasured stories in the Bible. Most stories are printed on two pages, a good length for the attention span of this age group. Included here are books from the Old Testament, such as Esther, Job, Song of Songs, Psalms, and the prophets Isaiah, Jeremiah, Amos, and Hosea. Ralph Milton provides an excellent selection of favorite stories of women and men in a contemporary storytelling format including many illustrations. Milton expanded this work into three volumes, *The Lectionary Story Bible,* Year A (2007), B (2008), and C (2009), (Kelowna, BC Canada, Woodlake Books). These volumes support those congregations that follow the appointed lectionary texts for Sundays in worship and/or in church school. One or two of the four lectionary texts are the focus with a style of storytelling that invites children into the text with their own questions. All three volumes use inclusive language for God, and the illustrations of Margaret Kyle invite the reader or hearer into the story, thus making this book accessible to nonreaders.

Included at the beginning of *The Family Story Bible* is a word for adults who are using this story Bible with children. Two statements provide insight into biblical interpretation and methodology behind this storybook. Milton writes, "The Bible is not a book of rules or a set of moral precepts that we somehow absorb and then order our lives by, although some contemporary churches encourage this view. Traditional Christianity says that when we're open to the 'word of God,' God will speak to us *through* the Bible. So I'm asking you to approach the Bible with a kind of childlike openness."[16]

This introduction provides a place of beginning for parents to consider their own assumptions about the Bible. Milton invites adults who want to read the Bible with children to remember that God still speaks to us through the Bible, and the Bible will never be boring.

Bible Animal Stories for Bedtime

This title by Jane Landreth (Uhrichsville, OH: Barbour Publishing, 2011) organizes its collection of stories by animals: "A Ram Is Provided" tells the story of the binding of Isaac. Jonah is told as two stories: "Jonah and the Big Fish," and "Jonah and the Little Worm." This is a small book and each story is told on three pages and concludes with a prayer. This would be a great beginning storybook for younger children. It will engage their imagination with the animals and it's just the right size for small hands to hold. I discovered it on a rack of books for sale at the grocery store!

Younger Elementary-Age Children—Ages Six to Eight

We know that developmentally, these children are growing in confidence of their new abilities. They can read, they are beginning to show interest and skills in particular activities (sports, music, art, dance, or drama). They bring their questions and curiosity to the Bible. This is a great time to continue to offer them biblical resources that will not only provide more content about the Bible but also invite their questions, the things they wonder about, and a chance to explore the cultural world in which it was written. With this kind of opportunity, they then are able to begin to make connections between the very old story of God's love for God's people and how it can relate to their lives right now.

Criteria for selection for a Bible storybook for this age group include:

- Content and choice of stories—which stories are selected? Are there stories of women and men?
- Additional resources for young readers—what additional content is available to the child to help her or him grow in understanding of the cultural worlds of the Old and New Testaments?
- Illustrations—what kind of illustrations are used? Are the illustrations good representations of what the characters would have looked like?

The Lion Read and Know Bible

This book (United Kingdom: Lion Children's Books, 2008) includes twenty-five stories from the Old Testament and twenty-four from the New

Testament. Though this is a small collection of stories, they are representative of the major characters of the Old Testament and the variety of kinds of stories included about Jesus in the Gospels portion of the New Testament: birth, teachings, parables, healing stories, death, and resurrection. The story of Pentecost, and one story of Paul and the book of Revelation, is all that is included for the rest of the New Testament.

The stories are short and appropriate for young readers. This story Bible is included for this age group because of the special articles that are included. For example, these resources provide additional information about nomads, Egyptians, the tent of worship in the Old Testament and the land of Jesus, and the Jewish faith in the time of Jesus in the New Testament. For the child who is curious about more background information, these twenty-eight short articles provide more information to help her or him grow in understanding about the cultural worlds of the Bible.

The Jesus Storybook Bible: Every Story Whispers His Name

This collection (Grand Rapids: Zondervan, 2007) has twenty-one stories from the Old Testament and twenty-three stories from the New Testament and is written by Sally Lloyd-Jones. This title is different from others in two ways. First, because the author wants the child who is hearing or reading these stories to understand that the Bible is "telling one Big Story," which is the story of God's love and centers on the story of a baby, and this connection is made very explicitly. So the story of the birth of Isaac in Genesis concludes with connecting it to the birth of Jesus. The story of Jonah who spent three days inside the fish is connected to Jesus's death and resurrection. A parent who is reading this book with a child should be prepared to understand the connection Jones is making between the Old Testament story and the life of Jesus.

This kind of storytelling is problematic in that it doesn't allow the stories from the Old Testament, the stories of God working through the Israelites, through prophets and storytellers, poets and musicians, to stand alone. Rather each story has what I call a "zip line" to Jesus. This kind of connecting can be confusing for a young child. Older children will be able to understand this theological move of the author of these stories.

Two additional distinctive traits of this storybook that make it worth considering are the creativity of the story titles and the way the stories are illustrated. For example the story of Jonah is titled "God's Messenger," which enables children to begin to understand that the story is about God sending a messenger (prophet) to the people of Nineveh. So many Bible storybooks title this story Jonah and the Big Fish, which doesn't help children get beyond the big fish, which is not the point of the story. The colorful and engaging artwork by an artist named Jago invites a child to wonder about the story through the illustrations and the graphic design, which place the illustrations sideways or across, or even around the page. Reading the stories becomes an adventure for a child! This book is available in English, Spanish, and Korean.

Shine On: A Story Bible

This book (Elgin, IL: Brethren Press, 2014) is the one of the newer Bible storybooks available for children and is designed to go with church school curriculum developed by the Mennonites. The New Revised Standard Version is the translation that is used for the stories, with 146 from the Old Testament and 156 from the New Testament. There are two distinctives that make this storybook unique. Each story is presented on two pages. The illustration is given more room than the story, which invites the reader into the story in strong visual ways. The illustrations are varied in form and style because of the different artists whose work is included.

The second thing that makes this storybook stand out is the use of three questions designed to invite the reader to wonder and reflect on the story, to explore it deeper to understand its meaning, and to connect the story with their own lives. In the introduction, the editors make it clear that they hope that their collection will be read and discussed in family settings at home and at the church.

The Bible for Children

This title (Intercourse, PA: Good Books, 2002) provides over two hundred stories retold for children. The introduction reminds the reader that the

Bible is a collection of different kinds of writings. Murray Watts, the author, offers his perspective on both the Bible and its appropriateness for children: "I have tried to reflect the magnificent breadth of this material, expressed in a rich variety of history, story and song. In my view, there is no need to limit younger readers to a cautiously edited and sentimental version. They will bring their own insights, questions and responses to these narratives."[17]

Elementary-Age Children—Ages Nine to Eleven

At this age, children are able to think abstractly, connecting stories from the Bible over time. They bring their growing curiosities to the stories and are able to ask thoughtful and analytical questions. The language art skills they are learning in school can be applied to reading the Bible. At this age, they are able to learn how to use simple maps, concordances, and dictionaries to help them access more information about the background and context of the Bible. They are ready to move from a Bible storybook to a whole Bible.

Deep Blue Kid's Bible

This book (Nashville: Common English Bible, 2012) is a children's version of the newest Bible to be translated, the *Common English Bible.* Three children, Asia, Edgar, and Kat act as guides to help children dive into the Bible. In addition to an introduction to each book of the Bible, there are in-text notes that help children understand and begin to connect with difficult and challenging biblical texts. Other features include maps, Bible exploration tools and facts, challenges for reading and remembering, and ways to connect text and life. All of these resources are written for children ages eight to twelve. Because the *Common English Bible* was written for an eighth-grade reading level or lower, the translation is very accessible for this age group of readers. Also available is an app, *Deep Blue Kid's Bible,* which includes many of the features in the print version as well as twenty-one puzzles from stories in the Hebrew Bible and New Testament. For more information, visit the website: www.deepbluekidsbible.com. There is even a church school curriculum centered around this children's Bible.

The Children's Illustrated Bible

This book (New York: DK Publishing, 2005) has stories by Selina Hastings and illustrations by Eric Thomas and combines several biblical resources into one volume. It includes an introduction to the Bible; overviews of particular time periods, such as the Patriarchs, Life in Egypt, Daily Life in Jesus Time, and the Early Church; and maps and a list of people named in the stories. Each story also includes side bar information that provides historic and cultural information. The kind of information that adults have to find with a concordance, Bible dictionary, or atlas are included here as well in a condensed version for children. The only drawback to this version is that the biblical quotes are from the King James Version. For the curious reader who wants more background about biblical stories, this is a great resource.

In addition to the books described above, there are several other titles that are excellent choices to have available in church school settings or on the minister or educator's shelf for use in worship with children.

The Pilgrim Book of Bible Stories

This storybook (Cleveland: Pilgrim Press, 2003) takes a very creative approach to the selection of included Bible stories. It is divided into nineteen chapters and includes stories from the laws of Leviticus, wisdom literature, and prophecy—the kinds of writings that are usually not included in children's Bibles. Each chapter includes an introduction "that reveals the developing thread of the story, linking history to interpretation, literature to life. This approach roots the stories in the historical reality of their times."[18] The other unique feature of this Bible storybook is the artwork, which was drawn by Diana Shimon, an Israeli artist who created her illustrations in Israel.

JPS Illustrated Children's Bible

These stories (Philadelphia: Jewish Publication Society, 2009) are retold by Ellen Frankel. In writing about her choices of the fifty-three stories that are included, Frankel says, "My stories were guided mainly by my sense of what makes a good story for children, but a few were included because they are pivotal to an understanding of the Jewish national story."[19] The illustrations by award-winning artist Avi Katz invite the reader into the drama and feelings of the stories. At the end of the book there is a concluding section, "Writing a Jewish Children's Bible: An Author's Notebook." Here the author provides the background for her selection: "My chief aim in writing this book has been to introduce American children to the language and rhythms of the Hebrew Bible."[20] Katz has adapted the stories from the 1985 JPS (Jewish Publication Society) translation. In this section she writes about how she wrestled with "objectionable or adult material" and why she included the binding of Isaac and the story of David and Bathsheba but not the rape of Dinah. She includes a section on gender and reminds the reader of the cultural context in which the Bible was written, and yet she states, "We cannot simply sweep aside the contradictions between the Bible's world and our own."[21] One way she chooses to address the issue of language for God is to use gender-neutral language.

Bible Storybooks

These books should be included in every church library. Rabbi Sandy Eisenberg Sasso takes favorite Bible stories for children and retells them in a midrash style, both filling in gaps in the story and, at the same time, inviting hearers or readers to connect the story with their lives. In this style of understanding biblical stories, an author like Rabbi Sasso searches out (literal meaning of *midrash*) the meaning of a text. "It is a way of reading into the text what may not be immediately apparent."[22] *Some* titles of books that Rabbi Sasso has written include: *Creation's First Light* (Indianapolis: IBJ Book Publishing, 2013), *In God's Name* (Woodstock, VT: Jewish Lights Publishing, 2004); *But God Remembered: Stories of Women from Creation to the Promised Land* (Woodstock, VT: Jewish Lights Publishing, 2008); *God's Paintbrush* (Woodstock, VT: Jewish Lights Publishing, 2004); *God In Between* (Woodstock, VT: Jewish Lights Publishing, 1998); *Noah's Wife: The Story of Naamah* (Woodstock, VT: Jewish Lights Publishing, 2002); *God Said Amen* (Woodstock, VT: Jewish Lights Publishing, 2000); *Cain and Abel, Finding the Fruits of Peace* (Woodstock, VT:

Jewish Lights Publishing, 2001); *Adam and Eve's First Sunset: God's New Day* (Woodstock, VT: Jewish Lights Publishing, 2003); *For Heaven's Sake* (Woodstock, VT: Jewish Lights Publishing, 1999).

The Read and Learn Bible

This Bible storybook published by the American Bible Society includes many stories, simply told with colorful illustrations. Most stories also include a brief textbox with information about some aspect of the story. This collection of stories would work well as a first storybook for young children.

The Mystic Bible

This title, published by Sophia Books in 2012, includes stories about Jesus from his birth through the Pentecost story. They are written by Alexandra Sangster in a poetry style that invites children to explore familiar stories through a new perspective. It is written for those who want the stories of the New Testament presented through word and image from a progressive perspective.

Bible Stories and Psalms for Young Children

These books offer just two examples of shorter storybooks that are useful both at home and at church. *Psalms for Young Children* (Grand Rapids, MI: Eerdmans Books for Young Readers, 2008) includes a collection of forty psalms retold for young readers by Marie Hélène Delval and illustrated by the artist Arno. They are simply paraphrased for children ages four to eight while "remaining faithful to the spirit of the biblical texts."[23] Imagine using one of these psalms in a call to worship! This same author also has a very small collection of nine stories from the Bible, *The Bible for Young Children* (Grand Rapids, MI: Eerdmans Books for Young Readers, 2008). They are retold simply with beautiful illustrations. This is a small storybook that would make a lovely gift for a young child. *Images of God for Young Children* (Grand Rapids, MI: Eerdmans

Books for Young Readers, 2008) invites children to explore the nature of God through a variety of images like joy, light, and wisdom.

Five-Minute Bible Stories

Lois Rock has retold twelve stories from the Old Testament and eight stories from the New Testament in *Five-Minute Bible Stories* (Minneapolis: Augsburg Fortress, 2005). Each story includes a very brief introduction and then tells the story with lovely illustrations by Richard Johnson. The Old Testament stories include: creation, Noah, tower of Babel, Abraham and Isaac, Joseph, Moses, Samuel, David and Goliath, Jonah and Daniel. The New Testament stories that she includes are: Jesus's birth, Jesus in the temple, Healing of the paralyzed man, the storm on the lake, lost sheep, good Samaritan, entering Jerusalem, and the story of the cross.

The Spark Story Bible

This is a book (Minneapolis: Augsburg Fortress, 2009) designed to be used by children in a church school setting. It is the storybook that goes with the children's curriculum *Spark*. It includes forty-five stories from the Old Testament and 105 stories from the New Testament. The introduction invites children and adults to "experience something new each time you read a story, either through the words of the story, the imaginative art, or in the face of the expressive caterpillar, Squiggles. Grow in faith together as you imagine, talk about, wonder and explore God's word."[24] Each story includes at least one sidebar invitation to connect with the story or connect the story with a child's life.

The Power Bible and *The Brick Bible*

There are two storybooks in the graphic illustrative style that are important to know about: *The Power Bible* (Irvine, CA: Green Egg Media, 2011) and *The Brick Bible* (New York: Skyhorse Publishing, 2011). Both use the graphic (comic book) style of illustrations. *The Power Bible* includes a statement from the artists who say that their intention was to use a comic book format to make it easier for people to read. There are ten books in the series, six for Old Testament and four for the New Testament. The stories follow the translation (New American Standard Bible) very closely and make clear that *The Power Bible* is not intended to be a substitute for a complete Bible. This would be a good collection to have available in church school classrooms as another example of how biblical stories are told and illustrated.

Another graphic style storybook is *The Brick Bible: A New Spin on the Old Testament* as told by Brendan Powell Smith. There are two volumes. Stories from the following Old Testament books are included: Genesis through Judges, Samuel, Kings and Chronicles. The New Testament stories are divided into the Gospels, Acts of the Apostles, and the Revelation of John.

The stories are described on the frontispiece as "original, modern interpretations of the Bible" that are based on the *King James Bible, Darby's Bible* (1890), and *Young's Literal Bible* (1862). The author also consulted modern English translations. The illustrations are photographs of the author's LEGO block recreations of the stories. His goal is "to present the Bible's content in a new, engaging, and fun way, and yet also to remain faithful to the way the Bible itself tells these stories."[25]

All stories are presented with graphic imagery, for example, the circumcision of Ishmael, the rape of Tamar, and all of the stories of battles between enemies. Rather than illustrations, the stories are represented with a sequenced setup of blocks.

The Stories They Are Hearing and Learning

The challenge of reading the Bible with children and youth is that we have to be comfortable with the questions they ask of the text. We have to be willing to say, "I don't know" or "Let's look that up together" or "What a great question, let's think about that together." Before we give a copy of *The Family Story Bible* to a child at her or his baptism or give the *Deep Blue Kid's Bible* to second graders, perhaps we should engage parents and other interested family members in some sessions together about what they will hear and read in the Bible. They need as much easing into the Bible as do their children.

THE CHALLENGE OF READING THE BIBLE WITH CHILDREN AND YOUTH IS THAT WE HAVE TO BE COMFORTABLE WITH THE QUESTIONS THEY ASK OF THE TEXT.

Ralph Milton provides a wonderful reminder for all us of how to read the Bible with children: "So enjoy each story, whether you think it is historically true, pure fiction, or somewhere in between. The inner truth, the wisdom, lives *inside* the story. Don't look for some pious little moral, but be open to a flash of insight into what it means to be spiritual human beings who live in families and communities with other spiritual human beings."[26]

Surely that is our hope and expectation in making the Bible both available and accessible to the youngest ones in our midst, that in hearing stories of God's people a long time ago, in reading poetry, in seeing the people that Jesus welcomed, we learn together what it means to live in this world. As the prophet Micah reminds us, all that God requires of us is "to do justice, embrace faithful love, and walk humbly with your God" (6:8).

CHAPTER FOUR

Stories That Form Us for a Life of Faith

From the moment religious teachers commence their task, they engage in the careful selection of data pertinent to the cognitively-based curricula they favor. Faith content quickly pushes spiritual awareness to the sideline. Soon children parrot, and eventually think, only within their inherited framework of belief. Faith, as a lively and ongoing encounter with "the More," becomes synonymous with the creeds and propositions of their particular religious tradition. As young people grow to rationally question, or even to reject, the validity of these formulations of truth, they are often left with no alternative for apprehending the spiritual realm of existence. Their spiritual repertoire remains flat and narrow.

—*T. Wyatt Watkins*

What is the alternative to a "flat and narrow" spiritual perspective? How do we help children build a faith vocabulary so that the home that they make for faith is roomy and spacious? How can we support children with their questions, their wonderings about the Bible? In what ways can we be attuned to a spiritual awareness of God's presence in their life, an awareness that will continue to grow with them? How can we help them draw on the Bible as a resource for their own life of faith?

In his book, *The Good Book: Reading the Bible with Mind and Heart,* Peter Gomes reminds us that it has been said that "most Christian adults live their lives off a second-rate second-grade Sunday school education, and that the more they hear of the Bible in church, the less they feel they know about it."[1] Even if this is true, it might be more correct to say a seventh- or eighth-grade Sunday school education since many youth "graduate" after their confirmation.

HOW DO WE HELP CHILDREN BUILD A FAITH VOCABULARY SO THAT THE HOME THAT THEY MAKE FOR FAITH IS ROOMY AND SPACIOUS?

It's no wonder then that adults who are formed like this and are now parents find it difficult to even read a Bible story with a child. Perhaps they think of this activity as only one of gaining knowledge and facts. As Watkins suggests, faith expression requires more than facts and knowledge. If a parent left church with a second-grade or seventh-grade church school education, then it's possible she or he has not spent time in wrestling with scripture, which is an important faithful activity.

Enabling a child's faith expression requires parents being able to be at home with their own faith, their own ways of spiritual expression, and their own practices of reading, wrestling with and interpreting the Bible. Biblical scholar Amy-Jill Levine writes about parables as stories that help us ask questions:

> Jesus knew that the best teaching concerning how to live, and live abundantly, comes not from spoon-fed data or an answer sheet. Instead, it comes from narratives that remind us of what we already know, but are resistant to recall.... It comes from stories that community members can share with each other, with each of us accessing the conclusions others draw, and so reassessing our own.[2]

Each time Jewish families eat a *shabbat* meal together or sit down for Passover, they remember and retell stories from the Bible and recall God's abiding presence in their life. *Shabbat* is intended as a place for sanctifying time. It begins with a prayer remembering the commandment to observe Sabbath and keep it holy. The Passover meal includes remembering the exodus narrative, retelling it with children so everyone grows up knowing and remembering. In such ways, Jewish children grow up living abundantly, experiencing the meaning of their faith at the table in their homes.

How do Christians celebrate Sabbath? In what ways do we observe the commandment to set it apart and make it holy? How do we support parents in this incredible opportunity for helping children grow in spiritual awareness? It is our job in the church to help adults gain confidence in their ability to read the Bible with their child. In this way both parent and child are blessed in a spiritual life that is rich and full, not flat and narrow!

The "Stuff" We Have Figured Out

Pastors and many church educators have had the privilege of a theological education. They also have experiences teaching the Bible, and are familiar and at home with resources like study Bibles, commentaries, and articles from websites such as workingpreacher.org or textweek.com. They have the ability and interest to keep up with current biblical scholarship. These practices enable them to approach the Bible with ease and confidence. They are able to wrestle with texts and are accustomed to making sense of biblical stories and how they can be heard, understood, and interpreted by a modern-day reader.

Pastors and educators and some lay leaders know the biblical narratives and are able to make sense of their meaning and connection to living a life of faith. The challenge is how to enable this ability in parents. Consider how the "stuff" we have figured out can be made accessible to a parent who simply wants help in how to read the Bible and read it with a child. This is not to say that pastors and educators have it all figured out, with all the answers, but rather that we have engaged in the process of sitting with text. Here's my "stuff" list. You may think of more to add. Each item on the list includes reference to a specific text and how it is interpreted in a children's Bible storybook or Bible.

I think that clergy and educators and lay people who like to read the Bible have done their own wrestling over the years and have answers to these six topics. It's important to think about how these topics can be engaged by parents. Each topic will be considered and then illustrated with examples from Bible storybooks.

1. How to Get Around in the Bible (Understanding Kinds of Writings, Authors, Etc.)

Clergy and educators feel at home with a Bible. Knowing where books are located, having a working knowledge of authors and styles of writing, and recognizing differences among the Gospels are all part of "the job" of teaching and preaching. Perhaps we have made it too easy for adults, providing pew Bibles so it's not necessary to even bring one to church on Sunday. And of course children and youth watch that. We give Bibles at different ages but are they ever brought back and used on Sunday or opened during the week? We have also made it easy by providing page numbers for the reading of the text in worship so no one ever has to look up a passage on their own or in a table of contents.

Although these simple practices can make scriptural study less intimidating for adults who did not grow up in a church environment, they are not supportive of family engagement with the Bible. But these practices of being able to find your way in the Bible, knowing about different kinds of writings, skills that church professionals sometimes take for granted can be shared and learned. It is helpful that children grow up learning basic information about the Bible, such as the organization into two testaments, Old and New, and a simple introduction to them. Equally useful is helping children learn that the Bible is a collection of sixty-six books, with different kinds of writing: law, history, poetry, prophecy, wisdom, gospels, letters, and apocalyptic literature.

Learning about the context and culture in which the Bible was written will be important as children grow in their abilities to read, analyze, and understand different kinds of writing. As children make the transition from hearing and reading individual Bible stories to becoming familiar with the Bible as a whole, these basic abilities will provide an important background.

Here are some examples from Bible storybooks. *The Lion Read and Know Bible* has an introduction to both testaments. It helps children understand about the first part of the Christian Bible, which includes stories of God's people who tried to follow God but often failed. But the Jewish people also knew that God loved them and forgave them. The New Testament is introduced as the second part of the Christian Bible that tells the stories of Jesus and his followers, people who also tried to follow and often failed. This story Bible has a small collection of stories but also includes notes that give children background information about the story. There are notes about "the tent of worship," "Solomon's golden Temple," information about the land where Jesus lived, and background about three great festivals celebrated by the Jews. These simple notes provide good background for a child, like a study Bible would for adults.

Candle Read and Share Bible is probably the simplest storybook to use with young children, as has been indicated before. Its organization also helps a parent learn with the child. *Candle* contains the stories that most church school curriculum includes for preschool and elementary-age children. Each division in the book includes a number of stories that are divided into smaller units, easy for telling or reading with young children. Stories from Genesis include: Beginning, Flood, Babel, and Abraham. Other stories included are Moses, Balaam, the Promised Land, Deborah, Gideon, Samson, Ruth and Naomi, Hannah, Samuel, David, Solomon, Elijah and Elisha, Joash, Hezekiah, Esther, Job, Daniel, Jonah, Isaiah, and Ecclesiastes. New Testament stories are grouped this way: Jesus's birth, boyhood, life, death, and resurrection; the sending of Holy Spirit; Paul; Peter; and Revelation.

The *Children's Illustrated Bible* includes a helpful introduction to the Bible at the beginning. With the sidebar notes included for each story, this story Bible truly becomes a study Bible for the reader, excellent for children and middle school youth. It has a wealth of facts and information that invite a child to want to know more.

Shine On is meant to be a storybook Bible for families to read together. The illustrations and the three ways children are invited to engage the story—Wonder, Connect, and Explore, help introduce the content and variety of writings in the Bible. The Old Testament portion includes some books not found in many other Bible storybooks: Job, Proverbs, six of the prophets, and three of the Psalms. "These stories present anew the exciting, curious, wonderful account of God at work in the world with flawed, genuine people."[3]

As you see, the authors of the Bible storybooks described here and in other chapters do a good job of story selection, choosing those they think are age appropriate for the reader. They vary with regard to how they introduce a child to the Bible as a whole. The kinds of writings, authors, time, and context are the types of information that are accessible to children as they age in their abilities and interest. The *Deep Blue Kids Bible* is the only complete Bible reviewed in this book. The introductions to each book and the variety of notes that are included support a child and a parent as they read the Bible together.

The *JPS Children's Illustrated Bible* is the only story Bible that includes anything about language for God. For some parents, inclusive language for God is important, helping their child to not grow up with only male images for God. This Bible, because it is the author's own translation, represents God as gender-neutral. The author writes, "To be fair to the Bible, we cannot impose our contemporary values of feminism and gender equality upon it. But to be fair to ourselves, we cannot simply sweep aside the contradictions between the Bible's world and our own."[4]

Many of the Bible storybooks reviewed here have made their own commitment to inclusion by telling many of the stories of named and unnamed women in the Bible. To read the stories of Esther and Miriam, Mary and Martha, and early church leaders such as Priscilla and Lydia are important for boys and girls as they begin to see the ways they are called to do God's work and be Jesus's disciple.

How to get around in the Bible is a skill that comes with practice. This we know! We need to offer parents the chance to grow confident in their skills so that they are comfortable opening and reading the Bible with their child. What if, instead of providing the page numbers for the text read in worship, we provided the time for everyone to locate it on their own. What if we began the church school year by inviting everyone to bring their own Bibles with them to church and use them during the reading of the texts? Perhaps this simple activity could help families grow in their abilities to feel at home finding their way in the Bible.

2. How to Interpret a Story

One of the skills that pastors and educators have is the ability to read a text and interpret its meaning, both as it was understood by the original audience and how we hear it in our context today. When you step back from a beloved Bible story known since childhood, it is important to ask questions such as, What is this story really about? How am I to make sense of something that is so hard to believe? What is it telling me about God?

The story of Noah in Genesis is often pictured as a mural on the walls of our preschool rooms. It shows the ark and usually a lot of the animals, marching two by two, and always a rainbow. But as you know a great deal happens between God's command to Noah to build an ark and the end of the story, when God makes a covenant with Noah and puts a bow in the clouds as a reminder that never again will floods destroy creation. The murals that introduce children to this story don't include the pictures that the artist Peter Spier included in his children's story, *Noah's Ark*. The pictures movingly show the story without words, the building of the ark, the animals walking on two by two, the closed door of the ark with the animals who were left standing there as the rain begins. The waters are rising up to the knees of the elephant and then the waters cover them. And a child knows without any words what happens.

WHEN YOU STEP BACK FROM A BELOVED BIBLE STORY KNOWN SINCE CHILDHOOD, IT IS IMPORTANT TO ASK QUESTIONS SUCH AS, WHAT IS THIS STORY REALLY ABOUT? WHAT IS IT TELLING ME ABOUT GOD?

We know that this story follows the story of Cain killing Abel. *The Bible for Children* begins the story of "A Flood and a Rainbow" by telling the reader that after Cain, many people also

> turned to violence—so much so that when God looked down upon the earth, he was filled with pain and sorrow. "I should never have made humankind," God said. "All they can think about is doing terrible evil."...God was angry at the ruin of his creation and said, "I will remove the people from the face of the earth—I will destroy this wickedness forever."[5]

And the floods came and destroyed the earth except for the Ark and all its inhabitants. As a promise that God will remember, a bow appears in the clouds. "'My rainbow,' said God, 'will remind you of my promise to you and every living creature. I will see it and I will remember the everlasting bond that I have made between me and all life on the earth.'"[6]

In *The Bible for Young Children* by Marie-Hélène Delval, Noah and the flood follows the story of creation, which concludes by reminding children that God gave the earth to humans so they can both live there and make it more lovely. This storybook does not include the story of Cain and Abel, so it makes the transition from Creation to Noah in this way. "But then people became mean, so mean that God was sorry that he had given them world. He wanted to destroy everything he had made. So God sent a flood to wash it all away."[7]

Bible scholars remind us that it is very likely that the two authors of the story of Noah (the Priestly and the Yahwist), which are combined in Genesis could have borrowed some parts from other ancient flood stories such as in the Gilgamesh epic. So the story of a flood that destroyed the earth was not unknown to the original audience hearing this story.

If we step back to wonder about what the story tells, we are reminded that "here at the height of the catastrophe (Gen 7:12-24), the two themes of the flood story converge. One is the deep human fear that order and life will collapse and disappear. The other is the deep human hope that life, like the animals and people aboard Noah's boat, will persevere and triumph in the end."[8]

These themes of fear and hope are common human experiences we all share. This story is also about loss—loss of life, loss of hope, loss of all that is familiar. And it is about recovery—regaining hope, recovery of life, new beginnings, a chance to start over. And it is a story about memory and promise.

As told by children's Bible storybooks, children can begin to build a vocabulary of faith by thinking about how God reacts to human activity. Older children will be able to look at the story from a literary point of view, comparing and contrasting the way the story is told by two different authors. Resources like the box of questions in *God's Big Story* help children think about the story in new ways. "Remember a time when something you made was ruined or broken and you had to start all over again. Wonder how God felt at having to start all over again."[9] A question like this one invites children to connect their own experience of loss and starting again with this ancient story.

As children age, they are able to think with their own observations and questions. Another card about Noah from *God's Big Story* box of questions helps a child think about how to interpret this story, how to make sense of something that seems unbelievable. "The whole earth won't be flooded again, but floods still do happen. When they do, people need help. Check online for information about recent floods. What can you do to help?"[10] This kind of affirmation will help younger elementary children who are concrete thinkers to continue their reading and engagement with this story.

Most children's Bible storybooks include a few parables, and the story of the Lost Sheep is always included. Luke 15 includes three parables, the Lost Sheep, Lost Coin, and Lost Son, which Luke turns into allegories about sin and repentance. In her book, *Short Stories by Jesus: The Enigmatic Parables of a Controversial Rabbi* biblical scholar Amy-Jill Levine invites us to rethink this parable with new understanding, letting go of negative stereotypes of Judaism and consider how the story would have been heard by its original audience without the editorial introduction by the author. A man has one hundred sheep and he realizes that he has lost one. He leaves the rest of the flock to go and find the one who is lost. After finding it, he brings it home and calls together his friends for a party to celebrate finding the lost sheep.

In Luke 15:7, the parable becomes an allegory with the statement about the lost one's repenting. As Levine points out, the allegory does not connect with the parable. "There was no repenting in the story; there was no sin; the sheep did not 'come to itself' and find its way home. It was the owner who lost the sheep, and if this losing were sinful, he's not seen repenting."[11]

The parable is told very faithfully to the text and the traditional interpretation in children's storybooks. In Lois Rock's *Five-Minute Bible Stories*, at the end of the story (which is both told and illustrated imaginatively), she includes Jesus saying that it's important to remember the celebration after the lost sheep has been found. "Because that's a bit like what happens in heaven when some wrongdoer makes that big change. When a wrong-doer finally sees that they're making a mess of their life and decides to put things right, you can almost hear the angels cheering."[12] Two storybooks provide a different emphasis with less of a connection between the parable and the allegory. *The Children's Illustrated Bible* cites both the Matthew and Luke accounts in the retelling of the story. In conflating this story, it includes the introduction to the parable from Luke and the conclusion from Matthew, "For it is the will of God that no one, however humble, shall be lost."[13] One of the sidebar notes provides information about how the Old Testament compares God's watchful care for the Israelites with a person who watches over all the sheep.

Shine On includes the story of the lost sheep and the lost coin with the title "Searching for the Lost." Children are invited to connect with the story by thinking about a time when they did something wrong and are reminded to remember they are loved by God always. The Explore sugges-tion also focuses on doing something wrong and being thankful for people who help us "make good decisions."[14] The focus of these suggestions seems to be less on the parable itself and more on the religious leaders.

Consider these interpretations for children in light of the comments from Amy-Jill Levine, who invites a second reading and hearing of this familiar story, freed from Luke's allegorical interpretation. She invites us to see what the parable is doing by noticing the owner. He has a large flock of sheep, one hundred to be exact, and when the owner loses one sheep, his flock is not complete. His rejoicing is rather amazing when you simply read the parable—all that partying because one sheep that he had lost is now found. The man looked at his sheep and counted, and noticed which sheep was not there. It was the absence of one that made his flock incomplete.

Levine asks this question, "When was the last time we took stock, or counted up who was present rather than simply counted on their pres-ence? Will we take responsibility for the losing, and what effort will we make to find it—or him or her— again?"[15]

Stripped of the allegory and allowed to stand on its own, as it would have been heard by the original Jewish audience, the parable also invites us in to hear and interpret it in new ways. With a new interpretation focused on the owner losing the sheep and realizing his flock was not complete, the story is reinterpreted no longer illustrating repentance but in a way that is more consistent with the title. The parable becomes a story about loss and recovery, sadness and joyous celebration.

We are invited to consider the question for us today. Who is lost to us? As we look around our congregations, who is present and who is missing? Whom do we welcome and assume will be there and who is no longer present? What about that family with an autistic child who is unable to participate in church school or worship without help? What about that teenager who simply falls off the radar after confirmation? Does anyone notice she is no longer attending? What about the widow who no longer has a beloved spouse to sit with and so sits at home alone on Sunday morning?

What if children were invited to wonder about the meaning of this parable with this suggestion? Think about a time in your life when you weren't included in a game or invited to a party. What did it feel like to miss out? Who do you know who might need to be included in your group of friends?

The kind of exegetical and interpretive work that Levine is doing invites us to read the parable as it is, stripped of editing by Luke. It does change the meaning and how we hear it and connect with it. For some, this change may simply not work because understanding the parable as a story about repentance is what is most important. But this new interpretation turns our thinking and understanding more to the middle of the parable, rather than the end. It asks us to look around and see who is present but not noticed. It asks us to consider whose presence is not with us and what are we going to do about it.

3. How to Wrestle with a Difficult Text

Bible scholar Phyllis Trible calls them texts of terror—those stories in the Bible we would rather not know were there, the stories we hope our children will not read: the rape of Tamar, Cain killing Abel, Hagar the servant sent away with her son, the daughter of Jephthah, and the daughters of Lot who were offered to a crowd of men.

We don't have to worry about children reading these stories, since they are not included in children's Bible storybooks. The most violent stories accessible to them are the binding of Isaac and the story of Jesus's death. We protect children from the more difficult stories. Then we give them complete Bibles, and the curious child who wants to read the whole book of Genesis, for example, will begin to read these stories and ask the questions we often don't know how to answer.

In choosing to wrestle with difficult texts ourselves, as adults, we become better able to hear and support children as they raise their questions. One thing is clear: the stories included in the Bible are no different from the stories that appear in any news cycle day in and day out. Conflict, wars, abuse, bloodshed, violence, sexism, racism are as much a part of our life as they were in the culture in which the Bible was written. The Bible was written to record events, to tell stories. Sometimes the stories are extremely difficult to read. Sometimes the connection to our life is clear, like with Jesus's teaching. Other times, we are left to make sense of a story on our own, like the story of Job or Jonah.

IN CHOOSING TO WRESTLE WITH DIFFICULT TEXTS OURSELVES, AS ADULTS, WE BECOME BETTER ABLE TO HEAR AND SUPPORT CHILDREN AS THEY RAISE THEIR QUESTIONS.

The connection between the biblical context and our contemporary context is that we still believe God is at work. We still believe that God who created, God who provided, God who restored, God who called forth faithful leaders, God who sent prophets to speak God's words—this same God—is still doing these same things today. Just like people in the Old Testament, we yearn to see God's face, to be close, to hear God's voice like Moses did.

When we wrestle with a difficult text, seeking to understand why this story is included in the Bible, we become more at home with asking questions of the text, with engaging it with our own wondering questions such as the ones described in chapter 2. When we approach difficult or challenging texts, we are then prepared to engage them with children.

Consider the story of the binding of Isaac, which is included in most children's Bible storybooks. The story (Genesis 22:1-19) appears in the Common Lectionary twice, as one of the readings for Holy Saturday and in Ordinary Time shortly after Pentecost. It is described as admired and troubling, gripping and chilling, one which presents a moral dilemma. We wonder what picture of God we get from this story—and the question we think but rarely verbalize: What kind of God would ask a father to sacrifice his son? And we also wonder, Would Isaac really have sacrificed his son if the Angel of the Lord had not intervened? And finally, it would be nice to be able to ask the author, Why was this story included?

Scholars tell us that an easy answer in telling this story is that it reminds the original audience that child sacrifice, which was practiced at some time in their history, was not required by the God of the Israelites. But there is more to the story than that. Because the story is told so sparely, we don't know what Abraham was thinking. Did he really believe that God would intervene? When Isaac asks, Where is the lamb for the sacrifice? the most common translation is, "God will provide." The *Common English Bible* translates it this way, "Abraham said, 'The lamb for the entirely burned offering? God will see to it, my son.' The two of them walked on together."[16] Another way to look at the story pushes beyond the obvious understanding of God testing God's leader, Abraham.

> Genesis 22 after all is a story of life coming into a situation of death; a story of redemption; a story of faith in the midst of extreme trauma. It is true that it sometimes is difficult to see God's provision and goodness in desperate situations when tragedy strikes. Nevertheless, the text calls upon us to look up and see God's goodness breaking into situations of despair. The true act of faith on the part of Abraham thus is not the blind faith that often has been the dominant message emerging from this text, but rather the ability to recognize God's provision in the ordinary, especially in those circumstances when everything appears to be futile.[17]

Often when a person of faith faces a difficult time in her life, you will hear her say, "God will provide." This simple affirmation of faith acknowledges a person's trust in God's care that is experienced in the ordinary experiences of daily life. "God will see to it" or "God will provide" was Abraham's response to Isaac when he asked about the sheep for the sacrifice. This simple response is a good example of what Timothy Beal describes as a cool text, one that is less defined, not providing much information, leaving gaps for the reader to wonder about. I wonder if Abraham was also thinking about how God would provide for his son, Isaac?

After the creation and the story of Babel, most children's storybooks then tell stories of the ancestors, beginning with Abraham and Sarah and the promise by God to them that they would have a child. Four storybooks include the troubling story of their beloved son, Isaac, told in Genesis 22.

The *Illustrated Children's Bible* from the Jewish Publication Society titles it, "The Binding of Isaac" and has an illustration showing Abraham, with a knife in his belt, walking in front of a teenage Isaac who is carrying the wood for the sacrifice. "The Sacrifice of Isaac" is the title in *The Children's Illustrated Bible*, which pictures Abraham kneeling beside a bound Isaac on the altar with the angel of the Lord telling Abraham not to harm his son. Also seen is the ram whose horns are caught in the bush. Information included in the sidebars tells about the location of this story and a picture of a ram caught in a thicket.

"God Tests Abraham" is how the story is titled in *The Bible for Children*. Unlike the two previous storybooks, this one fills in some of the gaps of the story, providing information about what Abraham was thinking. After Abraham tells the servants not to go with him and Isaac and promising they would return, it says, "He did not know how this would be possible. He did not know anything in the darkness of his own mind, but he trusted God."[18]

A similar style of storytelling that fills in gaps is used in *The Family Story Bible*, which gives it the title, "Abraham Doesn't Understand." *The Bible for Children* fills in the gap about what Abraham was thinking.

The Family Story Bible suggests what Isaac was thinking when he asks his father, Where was the lamb for the sacrifice? "Abraham seemed to take a long time to answer Isaac's question. Then he said, 'God will give us something for the sacrifice.' Isaac didn't understand, but he didn't mind. He often didn't understand the things his dad said about God."[19] The end of the story shows a picture of Abraham hugging his son. It connects the reader to the title with Abraham telling Isaac that he learned that this command of God was a test. "I also learned something else. God doesn't want us to hurt each other."[20]

The *Deep Blue Kids Bible* provides a note that asks the question, "Why did Abraham almost kill his son Isaac?" In this Bible for children, different kinds of notes are provided. Life Preserver notes help a child deal with difficult texts. This note begins this way, "If an adult you trust ever told you to do something you just didn't understand, you know a little about how Isaac and Abraham might have felt when God told Abraham to offer Isaac as a sacrifice."[21]

This kind of note, along with the paraphrased versions of the story included in *The Bible for Children* and *The Family Story Bible* provide help for both a child and a parent as they read this difficult story. *The Family Story Bible*'s title, "Abraham Doesn't Understand," could also include us as contemporary readers. We don't always easily understand old stories, why they are told, how they picture God, and how we are to make sense of them today.

4. How to Rethink a Well-Known Story in New Ways

Sometimes stories we read in the Bible are too familiar. By that I mean, we have heard them for so many years, we wonder what new thing can we possibly hear in this text. This is a great example of why the wondering model of bringing questions to the text is so helpful. It enables a child and even an adult to see the possibilities for new understandings and interpretations, appreciating the narrative and all its richness rather than reading for information.

THE WONDERING MODEL OF BRINGING QUESTIONS TO THE TEXT ENABLES A CHILD AND EVEN AN ADULT TO SEE THE POSSIBILITIES FOR NEW UNDERSTANDINGS AND INTERPRETATIONS, APPRECIATING THE NARRATIVE AND ALL ITS RICHNESS RATHER THAN READING FOR INFORMATION.

Consider these well-known stories, ones which are almost always included in children's Bible storybooks: the birth of Jesus and the parable of the Good Samaritan.

The birth of Jesus is recorded in two Gospels: Matthew and Luke. One of the things that is apparent when reading the birth stories is that our retelling of this event is probably influenced by popular Christmas carols. Often this story is conflated in our memories, that is, we put the two birth stories together, making it sound as one. In Luke's account, we get more of the story of Mary, her visit by the angel, and her visit with Elizabeth. Jesus's birth is told simply, followed by the visit of the shepherds. The story of the Magi and King Herod is Matthew's story.

The *Deep Blue Kids Bible* has a "Did You Know?" text box that provides a bit more information for the child who is reading about what Mary did after Jesus's birth when she "wrapped him snugly." The note reminds the reader that wrapping a child in this way make "the baby feel safe and warm."[22] Contrast "snugly" with the more often translated "swaddling clothes."

Luke 2:7 ends with the explanation about where Mary was giving birth to Jesus. She "laid him in a manger, because there was no place for them in the guestroom."[23] This may sound odd because of growing up and always hearing the word *inn*, which makes the reader think not about a home but about a place where a traveler would stop for the night. In fact, a guestroom was an extra room in a person's house, much like some of us have in our houses today. The note on this verse in the *Common English*

Study Bible suggests that "Jesus was born in borrowed space, previewing the nature of his ministry."[24]

The *Candle Read and Share Bible,* a good story Bible for young children, divides this story into ten parts beginning with the Luke account of the visit of the Angel to Mary and following the Luke text fairly closely, concluding with the visit of the Magi and the journey of the family to Egypt, which is told in Matthew's account. The birth story, taken from Luke, pictures Jesus wrapped very snugly in the stable, noted as a place for animals. "And that's where God's Baby Son was born. His first bed was on the hay in the box where the animals were fed."[25] The note in the textbox at the bottom of this page asks, "Why do you think God would want His Son to be born where the animals were kept?"[26]

Here is a great example of how a familiar story known by most adults and children invites continued wondering and reflection as a reader hears it in a new translation and with questions that invite the reader to go deeper into the story. How interesting that the note in the study Bible that connects the place of Jesus's birth with the focus of his ministry is implied in the question asked for children in the *Candle Read and Share Bible.*

The story of the Good Samaritan told in Luke 10:25-37 is surely the most well-known parable that Jesus taught, still referenced today. "Good Samaritan" stories are popular news items in the face of an increasingly violent world. In Luke, Jesus tells it to answer the question of a lawyer who wanted to know how he could live with God forever. When Jesus asked him what scripture had to say, the lawyer correctly quoted from Deuteronomy 6:5. But then the lawyer asked Jesus, "Who is my neighbor?" And Jesus told him the parable of the Good Samaritan.

Everyone seems to know the basic story. It's one we've heard all our lives, and we get it. We know who the good guy is, the Samaritan who stops to help the injured man. We know that Samaritans and Jews were more like enemies than friends. And we get the point of Jesus's telling of the story. The Samaritan is the one who acts like a neighbor and that's what Jesus wants us to do. Oftentimes we stop here but the story continues. Jesus then asks the lawyer, "What do you think? Which one of these three was a neighbor to the man who encountered thieves?" (Luke 10:36).

It's fairly simple, a question and an answer, but Jesus's answer can be explored and understood in more depth than we have usually interpreted it. As Amy-Jill Levine suggests in her book *Short Stories by Jesus*, understanding this parable and its meaning requires more than seeing it as a nice moral lesson about helping someone in need. The Samaritan not only helped the injured man, he provided the resources for his recovery and the costs of this continued care. "Thus the sense of loving neighbor means continual action, not something to check off the to-do list. . . . The issue for Jesus is not the 'who' but the 'what,' not the identity but the action. . . . For the lawyer, and for Luke's readers, the Samaritan does what God does."[27] And the lawyer is told by Jesus to do the same as the Samaritan. And we are left to wonder what the lawyer did in response.

What did Jesus want his hearers to understand? Jesus asks the lawyer, "What do you think? Which one was a neighbor?" The *CEB Study Bible* note invites readers to think more deeply about Jesus's meaning in telling this story. "This is the real question for Jesus' followers, not 'Who is my neighbor?' but 'Who behaved like a neighbor?'" Jesus hoped the lawyer would understand that living with God meant that you lived not with just an identity of a neighbor who shows mercy to others but a neighbor who always lives in every action with mercy and kindness toward others.

In reviewing children's storybooks, we see that most simply tell the story as we know it. A very few get close to an understanding of this story being about actions of a neighbor, not just identity. Desmond Tutu's *Children of God Storybook* concludes the telling of the story with Jesus reminding the lawyer that he was a part of the same family as the Samaritan. The prayer that Tutu includes invites the children to love their enemies and to recognize them as a part of their family.

In *The Family Story Bible*, Ralph Milton does the best job of any of the storybooks in his paraphrase of this story for children. The Samaritan not only helps get the injured man to a safe place but he promises to return and check up on him and pay for any additional expenses. "Here is some money to pay for it. I'll come back in a few days. If it costs any more to take care of him, I'll pay you."[28] The lawyer is left with much to think about when Jesus tells him that being a neighbor means being like the Samaritan. "Go and be like that kind of person."[29]

The Augsburg Story Bible will often capture a meaning of a text through the illustrations. Readers are invited to wonder about this story as they look at the picture of the injured man. The person pictured tending to his wounds is Mother Theresa, a woman who certainly lived her life as a neighbor to all, offering her mercy, kindness, and love. Connecting this very old story to the contemporary culture of children today is a great way to help them hear, understand, and make connections. It would be interesting to explore this story with children using questions:

- I wonder why the Priest and the Levite didn't stop to help?
- I wonder what the Samaritan and the injured man talked about?
- I wonder how you have acted like a neighbor to someone else?

5. How to Make Sense of Stories That Are Hard to Believe

In 2012, the Smithsonian displayed Thomas Jefferson's Bible, which has been described as a "cut and paste" Bible since he evidently took a Bible and cut out the parts he thought were not central to teachings about Jesus. Jefferson's Bible, published in 1820, was titled, *The Life and Morals of Jesus of Nazareth.* His process was quite methodical, comparing six translations written in Latin, Greek, French, and King James English.[30] Finding the teachings of Jesus to be important and of value, he was concerned about how they were interpreted by the Gospel writers. One of his criteria were stories that he considered to be "contrary to reason" so he took out his trusty blade and eliminated miracle stories, thus creating his own version that author Stephen Prothero has called "scripture by subtraction."[31]

Authors of Bible storybooks don't share Jefferson's concern. They include a variety of miracle stories for children to read, often with very little help provided for interpretation. Abraham and Sarah were childless and quite advanced in age when God promised them a child, a story similar to Elizabeth and Zechariah told in Luke. The Israelites enslaved in Egypt were promised freedom and the Promised Land. After plagues and the first Passover, they followed Moses and Miriam to the edge of the Reed Sea, and when the waters parted, they made their escape.

The miracles that Jesus performed, from walking on water, to making a boy's lunch multiply to feed a crowd, from turning water into wine at a party to healing people from disease and illness, cause a modern-day reader to pause and ask, Did this really happen? They invite a child to ask, Do miracles happen today?—a question the parent probably wants to ask as well.

THE MIRACLES THAT JESUS PERFORMED CAUSE A MODERN-DAY READER TO PAUSE AND ASK, DID THIS REALLY HAPPEN? THEY INVITE A CHILD TO ASK, DO MIRACLES HAPPEN TODAY?

Healing stories are always included in Bible storybooks. One exception I found is that none are included in *The Lion Read and Know Bible*, which is really an excellent storybook, appropriate for young children/readers. It's interesting to speculate about why they are not included. Rational minds read a Bible story and ask the question, How did that happen? Children read about Jesus healing someone and then include a family member or friend in their prayers, asking God to heal the person.

I was getting ready to lead a workshop at a local congregation on children and faith, when a woman came up and gave me a list of questions from her daughter. One question asked, Do miracles happen today in the same way they did in the Bible? I hope so. I think she verbalized a question we all ask. There are many stories in the Bible that are simply hard to imagine, especially if we read them as literal—the story of the Israelites led by Moses and Miriam through the Red Sea, or the story of Jonah. And then there are a myriad of stories of miraculous events and healings told in the Gospels.

We have some choices. We can follow Jefferson's model and create our own cut-and-paste Bible, or we can take the Bible as a whole, knowing that if we were to tell the stories today of God's call to God's people, it would probably include the same kinds of stories of the reality of life, hardships, and miracles we can't explain, and healings—of bodies, minds, souls, attitudes. Perhaps this is the way we help parents and their children wrestle honestly with the whole Bible.

Consider two stories from the New Testament that are good examples of how we can wrestle with stories that are hard to believe. The healing of the woman who touched Jesus is found in Mark 5, Luke 8, and Matthew 9, where it is told within the story of the healing of Jairus's daughter. This unnamed woman had been bleeding for twelve years and despite spending considerable money on doctors, she was still sick. She had heard about Jesus and when he came to her village, she reached out and touched his clothes. And she was healed. Jesus turned, knowing what had happened, and asked who had touched him. When the woman came forward, he acknowledged that it was her faith that had healed her.

The story is remarkable for several reasons. She is a woman who is alone. She has no male family member to help her and so boldly appears in the crowd and reaches out to touch Jesus, believing that she could be healed, and it was so. Equally unusual is that her healing was not in response to Jesus's action, rather it came at her own initiative, as biblical scholar, Frances Taylor Gench, suggests: "She does not request healing. Instead she violates social codes and perhaps even religious law to claim healing for herself, without permission from anyone—without even the compliance of Jesus."[32] This is the only healing story in Mark where this happens. Evidently Matthew was not comfortable with healing happening without the initiative of Jesus so he changes that fact in his telling of the story.

Another interesting fact about the woman is that we never hear her voice in direct speech. Gench points out tactile imagery, how the word *touch* is used four times, and how in Mark, women are physically present in touch, rarely in speech. In this story, the woman's actions speak volumes. Would that we could have heard this story with her voice!

"The Woman Who Touched Jesus" is told in *The Bible for Children*, closely following the Mark version. It does give voice to the woman when she responds to Jesus's question. "'Lord, I was afraid . . . I . . . please forgive me. I only wanted to touch you and . . .' Jesus took her hand. 'Daughter,' he said, 'your faith has healed you.'"[33] The illustration shows several feet walking and a glimpse of the woman reaching out, touching the bottom of Jesus's robe.

The Children's Illustrated Bible provides all three Gospel sources of this story but follows the account from Matthew where the woman's healing is in response to Jesus's pronouncement. The illustration shows Jesus standing in front of a large group of men with the woman bending over touching the bottom of his clothes. "Two Miracles in One Day" is the title in *The Read and Learn Bible.* It, too, follows Matthew and shows Jesus speaking to the woman as Jesus pronounces her healing and blessing.

"The Woman Who Touched Jesus" is the title of Ralph Milton's retelling of the story from Mark in *The Family Story Bible.* He fills in the gaps of the story and gives voice to the silent woman. When Jesus asks who touched him, she replies, "Don't be angry with me. . . . I've been sick for so long. I needed your help." Jesus replies, "I'm not angry. . . . I'm happy. You are very brave. You trust God's love. You won't be sick anymore. Go in peace."[34]

As word about Jesus's healing and teaching spread, more and more people came to see him, to get close. Gench reminds us that the one who was intent on helping people see how to live, how to love, whom to include, was often interrupted. "Jesus allows himself to be interrupted by a nameless, destitute woman who deters his mission to a prominent religious official." We sit with this text and we sit with our lives. Do we dare to let the interruptions shape our compassion and loving presence with others, even a child?

The story of Jesus walking on water to reach his disciples who were in trouble on a boat is told in Matthew 14, Mark 6, and John 6. It follows the story of the feeding of the five thousand. Matthew adds the response of Peter who asks to meet Jesus on the water. And Mark's version concludes with the author commenting on the fear of the disciples in Mark 6:52:

"That's because they hadn't understood about the loaves. Their hearts had been changed so they resisted God's ways."

The Children's Illustrated Bible follows the story from Matthew and shows Jesus reaching out to Peter who is sinking in the water. *Candle Read and Share* follows the story from Mark and shows Jesus walking on the water toward the disciples in the boat. The note for the children asks, "If you had been in that boat, what would you have done?"[35]

The Read and Learn Bible provides all three references for the story but conflates the story using Mark and Matthew. The basic story of Jesus responding to the cries of the disciples and walking on the water to reach them, as it is told in Mark and John, is pictured. The story concludes with Matthew's ending where the disciples acknowledge that Jesus is the Son of God.

"Walking on Water" in *The Bible for Children* tells the story following Matthew's account. Adding details to the story, the reader is quickly able to grasp the disciples' fear, first in facing the strong winds on the lake and then in seeing Jesus walking toward them. The vivid illustration captures this sense of both fear and awe. This version also fills in gaps by adding some of Simon's thinking. In response to Jesus's question about his doubt, "Simon knew there was no blame, just that simple question which rang in his ears for many years to come: Why did you doubt?"[36]

Shine On invites children to connect with the story by thinking about times when they have been afraid. "The next time you're afraid, breathe slowly and invite Jesus to calm your heart."[37]

As difficult as it is, I wouldn't want Jefferson's "Bible by subtraction." I'm glad that children's Bible storybooks don't shy away from miracle stories. Children concerned with concrete analysis may totally believe there is no way Jesus could have done this. Others may joke about big rocks underneath the water that no one could see! Some may admit that miracles happen every day. A parent would walk through fire and raging water to save the life of a child. Every day there is a good news story about someone doing the miraculous, like searching for life after an earthquake and not giving up for three days and then finding someone who is alive.

As adults, we read the miracle of the woman who touched Jesus and was healed. And with children, we offer our prayers to God for healing of people whom we know and love. Do miracles happen? There are so many ways to answer—*I don't know, what do you think? Yes, but not in the ways they did in the Bible. Or, absolutely, miracles happen every day.* Miracles happen when people believe that love and mercy are infinitely strong. Miracles happen when we believe that God's presence is near. Miracles happen when we are able to make it through the challenges of loss and pain. Miracles happen when God's presence and love are with us through the lives of those who are near to us with comfort and love.

WHEN WE ENGAGE THESE STORIES WITH OUR OWN WONDERING QUESTIONS AND ENCOURAGE THOSE QUESTIONS IN CHILDREN, THEN WE BECOME BETTER ABLE TO HEAR AND READ THE WHOLE BIBLE, NOT A SUBTRACTED ONE!

We are able to make sense of stories in the Bible that seem hard to believe to a contemporary reader when we translate these stories from an ancient context into the contemporary world in which we live. When we engage these stories with our own wondering questions and encourage those questions in children, then we become better able to hear and read the whole Bible, not a subtracted one!

6. How to Get an Understanding of God and God's Hopes for Humankind: Essential Teachings of the Bible That Will Grow with Children

Reading the Bible can be a rather daunting task. With so many kinds of writings, readers often want to know, What's the story line? Is there a thread that runs throughout the Bible that connects the testaments? Or, when thinking about reading the Bible with children, What do we hope they will wonder about, question? What connections do we hope a child will make about how she or he can live as a faithful Christian?

Most pastoral leaders probably have a list of such texts that are central to understanding how God, Jesus, and God's Spirit are revealed in the Bible. Parents bring their children to church school and midweek programs to learn the stories of the Bible and how they connect with their life today. Church school curriculum focuses on many of the same stories included in children's Bible storybooks. Both the curriculum and Bible storybooks introduce children to treasured stories of familiar characters in the Old Testament and the stories of Jesus and the beginnings of the church. As children develop from thinking concretely to being able to think abstractly, their abilities to interpret texts grow with them. As they move from elementary to middle school and high school, they are able to see the larger picture of the Bible and wrestle with meanings.

It is possible for a child's knowledge about God as revealed in Bible stories to be the foundation for his or her spiritual awareness. The seeds for seeing threads or themes that are present in the Bible are planted early as a child is introduced to story. Look again at the quote at the beginning of this chapter. It is possible for a child's knowledge about God as revealed in Bible stories to be the foundation for his or her spiritual awareness. One does not have to exclude the other.

Consider these stories as foundational to a child's life of faith. You may have different ones on your list.

Life Includes Both Happy Times and Sad Times

The book of Ecclesiastes, a part of the section of the Bible known as wisdom literature, wrestles with what is most important in life. The most familiar passage is from Ecclesiastes 3:1-8, the verses about time. It's rare for children to be introduced to the kind of writing we know as wisdom literature. Yet the verse from Ecclesiastes about time is certainly appropriate for the culture in which we live.

Children are not immune from feelings of sadness. Young children don't always have the words to express what they are feeling, but we know that they experience life just as we do and that there are times when things are going well and there are times when things are going badly. The verses in Ecclesiastes remind us of both sides of life, and the contrasts the author uses provide vivid imagery for how we can live.

The *Candle Read and Share Bible* for young children is the only storybook in the ones I reviewed that includes this text from Ecclesiastes. In two pages, it presents a brief synopsis of the verses reminding children that in our lives, there will be both happy times and sad times. The text box reminds children that "a little bit of everything happens in our lives. The important thing is to stay close to God all the time."[38]

In the *Deep Blue Kids Bible*, the "God's Thoughts/My Thoughts" note reminds children that sometimes it's hard to know what to do, that it's important to listen to wise people, those who can help us follow God. It concludes in this way: "Who in your life do you consider to be wise? Ask God to help you grow in wisdom."[39]

These verses are important for children and adults as they face life and everything that happens. Children who grow up knowing that God is present with them when difficult or bad things happen are able to make it through and celebrate when good things come their way. God is present with him when a grandparent dies and their pastor spends time with him and listens to his stories. God is present with her when her friends visit her when she is sick. Children who grow up with the spiritual awareness of God's presence in all things have the ability to face life and all of its challenges.

God's Voice

It's such a common yearning, to want to hear God's voice, so that we know the right thing to do. The Old Testament has stories of people who also shared this desire.

A few of the Bible storybooks that have been examined here include prophetic literature. The words of prophets that are found in story Bibles include Elijah, Jonah, Isaiah, Micah, Amos, Jeremiah, and Zechariah. It is interesting to see what verses are chosen to illustrate God's word to God's people, then and now.

The story of the prophet Elijah who challenged King Ahab's prophets of Baal is told in 1 Kings. After God told Elijah to kill the prophets of Baal, King Ahab's wife, Jezebel, threatened to kill Elijah, so he ran for his life to Mount Horeb. There God finds him and invites him to come out on the side of the mountain, and God passes by. The *Augsburg Story Bible* titles this, "Elijah Hides." The *JPS Children's Bible* and *The Bible for Children* title this story "The Still, Small Voice." And *The Family Story Bible* calls it "God Speaks in a Whisper."

In 1 Kings 19:11-12 we read that Elijah did not hear or see God in the wind, earthquake, or fire but rather in "a still, small voice," (KJV) or in the "sound of sheer silence" (NRSV), or in a "sound. Thin. Quiet" (CEB). "When Elijah heard God's voice, he felt strong enough to keep on being a prophet."[40]

We teach children about the importance of making good decisions, about doing the right thing. The story of the prophet Elijah reminds us of a person who was doing the right thing but it got him in trouble. He ran to get away from everything and probably even tried to hide from God. But he found out that was impossible. We help children grow in their spiritual awareness when we teach them how to pause, to listen for God's voice helping them make right choices, wise decisions. And we teach them that they may need to listen carefully, because it might come in a whisper from a parent, or in the small voice of a friend who helps them do what is right.

Living as One Committed to Living with Justice and Peace for All

It starts early in life, as soon as a two-year-old says, "No, it's mine." Children learn early one of the most difficult things in life: how to share, how to get along with others. How good it is that, now, children are taught in school how to handle difficult situations, how to listen, learn to compromise, and mediate so conflicts don't escalate into violent confrontations. Learning how to live with people who are different from us, learning about other religions, the ways that others worship God, all of these experiences help a child experience God's intention for the world, that we live and enjoy it and each other peaceably.

A challenge in reading the Bible is holding together the complexities, the paradoxes. The Old Testament is full of violent stories, of war and unimaginable atrocities, and these stories are told in great detail. Just like today, people in these stories fought about land and religion. Yet we also know that when we come to the prophets, toward the latter part of the Old Testament, we hear a strong prophetic voice for peace.

A CHALLENGE IN READING THE BIBLE IS HOLDING TOGETHER THE COMPLEXITIES, THE PARADOXES.

The Read and Learn Bible offers young children a synopsis of the prophet Micah's words from chapters 4 to 5. God's message of hope that God wanted Micah to tell was that "one day the fighting would end. All the weapons of war would be turned into rakes and shovels. People would never again make war or attack one another."[41]

The Bible for Children and *The Read and Learn Bible* both include the prophecy of a shepherd who would come from Bethlehem to lead his people and bring peace. *The Bible for Children* also includes verses from Isaiah 9, with the title "The Promised King," about the one who would be known as the Prince of Peace. *The Family Story Bible* quotes these same verses with this introduction: "Sometimes Isaiah talked about a special leader who would show the Hebrew people how to love God."[42]

The Family Story Bible includes a very simple synopsis of Isaiah's message. "Stop doing wrong things. Learn to do right things. Try to be fair to other people. Help those who are sad or who are hurting. Help people who are sad or who are hurting. Help people who don't have anyone to look after them."[43] By introducing a prophet to a child as someone who listens for God, the child becomes able to connect the words of the prophet a long time ago with our actions today.

Shine On: A Story Bible includes Isaiah 65:17-25, the familiar passage about the prophet's vision of peace where all of God's creation will live together peacefully. The "Connect" question invites a child to connect the vision of Isaiah with their own dreams by asking, "What are your dreams for the world?"[44]

Amos and Micah were two prophets whose words are often heard and quoted. Amos was a farmer when he was called by God. He noticed the disparity between rich and poor and he became God's prophet of justice. His image of justice rolling down like a river and righteousness like an ever-flowing stream were often quoted by Dr. Martin Luther King Jr., as he prophetically called God's people to change laws that denied persons of color their civil rights. *The Family Story Bible* puts Amos's words in the language a child can understand. "This is what I want. I want justice. I want justice when everybody is fair to everyone else. I don't want you to hurt other people or take things away from them. I want you to be kind to everyone."[45]

Shine On includes the words from Micah 6:1-8. Here children are introduced to the things that make God happy. It is not lots of things or burnt offerings but to do what is good—"do justice, love kindness and walk humbly with God." In response to the words of Amos and Micah, *Shine On* asks children to think about a situation that they know of that is unfair and what they should do about it. This storybook concludes the Old Testament with Zechariah's vision of the world that God wanted. It's a city where everyone lives together peacefully, where God's covenant with God's people is lived out. The Old Testament begins with God's creation and plan for the world, and it closes with a vision and that has not dimmed in God's eyes.

Loving God and Loving Neighbor

Jesus summed it up well when he answered the lawyer who asked him, How can I always live with God? Jesus reminded him of the great commandment from Deuteronomy 6, to love God with everything we are and have. And Jesus added to that, to also love our neighbors, as much as we love ourselves. Living in the world today, there may be no stronger imperative, then, than loving our neighbors. It requires us to think about who our neighbor is and what it means to show love.

With the stories of Jesus told in Bible storybooks, children are invited to make the connections between teachings and practices of faith. The command to love God and love neighbor can be understood with very concrete examples. Choosing which stories to highlight here is totally subjective, of course. Everyone has their favorites. Two are included here because of the ways they are told in a variety of Bible storybooks.

Hearing texts frequently is an important way that stories from the Bible become familiar and embedded in our lives of faith. Words that are often spoken at the invitation to communion are taken from the story of the disciples walking on the road to the village of Emmaus. The two disciples, who are not mentioned in the Gospel, are talking about the recent events. As they walk, the risen Jesus joins them, but the disciples "were prevented from recognizing him" (Luke 24:16). The disciples were surprised that their fellow traveler had not heard about the details of what happened after the death of Jesus. Jesus reminded them of the stories of Moses and the prophets, why Christ came and died.

The disciples, concerned for Jesus's safety on the road, insist that he stop with them and share a meal. In the breaking and blessing of the bread, "their eyes were opened and they recognized him" (Luke 24:31). Jesus disappeared from their sight and they were left to reflect on what had happened. They returned to Jerusalem, eager to share what had happened in their experience with the risen Lord.

This story is found in four storybooks. Both *The Family Story Bible* and *Lion Read and Know* retell the story, simplifying the text and adding some dialogue. For example, in Jesus's response to the disciples, he says, "Our holy books talk about the messiah, after all, and they do say that he will have to suffer before his kingdom really comes into being."[46] In *The Family Story Bible*, Cleopas recognized Jesus when he recalled how Jesus had a last supper with the disciples and had broken bread with them at the table.

The *Candle Read and Share Bible* includes this story in the section with stories about Jesus's death and resurrection. There are ten about his death and five about his resurrection and post-resurrection appearances. Because this storybook is focused for young children, the story is greatly simplified, offering the barest of details, omitting what they were talking about. Two pictures show the three men walking and then eating together as Jesus breaks the bread. The textbox invites the children to wonder about why the disciples were so surprised when they met Jesus on the road.

Shine On storybook invites children to wonder about the change in emotions of the disciples, how sad they were when they began the road trip and how happy they were on their return to Jerusalem. Children are invited to connect with the story with the suggestion that it's good to talk with others whenever we are upset or confused.

The scene of the disciples recognizing Jesus in the breaking of bread is a reminder for us, too. Beyond the communion table, we move out to other tables at home, at school, at picnics in the park. Wherever we are we have the opportunity to keep our eyes open, recognizing the moments and places where the teachings of Jesus about love, about hospitality, about caring for others—need our hands for implementation.

Beatitudes

Another text is so familiar to our ears that we can say it. The Beatitudes are one of the earliest and important teachings of Jesus found in both Matthew and Luke. Jesus lifts up those who are poor in spirit, those who mourn, the meek, the pure in heart, and those who work for peace. "Blessed are" is the translation in the New Revised Standard Version. The Common English Bible translates it, "Happy are..." This teaching comes after Matthew 4:17, which gives us a clue about what Jesus's ministry was going to focus on: "Change your hearts and live! Here comes the kingdom of heaven."

A familiar response to the question, How are you? is, I'm blessed! One way to understand what it means to be blessed is to trace its meaning from the Old Testament. Psalm 1 begins by describing the truly happy person. The Hebrew word for "happy," *ashar,* has the literal meaning of going on or advancing, or finding the right way ahead. So with all the myriad ways Jesus could begin his ministry, he begins with promises that you will be blessed and then connects these blessings with the very real human experiences of mourning, meekness, hunger and thirst, mercy, and working for peace.

Consider two Beatitudes. "Blessed are the poor in spirit for theirs is the kingdom of heaven." How do you tell people that being poor in spirit is a blessing? And what does it mean to be poor in spirit? On first glance, one would not think of this as a positive thing. But reframe it. As biblical scholar, Dr. Amy Oden, has noted, "poverty of spirit bears within it the blessing of life abundant." Think about it in terms of being "emptied, [being] free of clutter, available and roomy."[47] So the reversal here is with the word *poor*. "When we are 'wealthy in spirit,' we are full of ourselves, eager to display how much we know, how much we can do. Or we are filled up with multi-tasking, preoccupied by busy-ness."[48] What room is there left for the work that God can do? "Blessed, then, are the poor in spirit, these ones not so full of themselves. They show us open lives, available for the mercy that re-orders life."[49] Those whose spirits are roomy and available are on the right road.

A second blessing is for those who mourn, for they will be comforted. The most obvious interpretation is that when we mourn, when we grieve loss in our lives, we will be comforted. How many times have you said this blessing to another? This blessing, too, can be reframed. Consider this Beatitude from the context in which Jesus was teaching. The Gospel writer, Matthew, would like for us to remember that mourning also relates to how far the present life is from that which is God's vision. Those who mourn when they see injustice, those who mourn when racist or homophobic comments are made, and those whose mourning turns into action on behalf of others are blessed by God.

Adults find these blessings hard to understand, so how do we read them to children? *The Children's Illustrated Bible* has a sidebar text note telling readers that the word *beatitude* means "blessing," and that the Beatitudes describe the qualities of a person who tries to live in the ways that Jesus taught. *Shine On* invites children to reflect on several of the Beatitudes, to wonder about their meanings. With the title "Jesus Teaches," *The Family Story Bible* interprets the Beatitudes for children. "If you feel very small inside, Be happy. God's love is yours. If you feel very sad inside, Be happy. God will help you feel better."[50]

The *Augsburg Story Bible* includes two illustrations for the Beatitudes that invite the reader to make the connections between this ancient text and its relevance for a modern world. In one picture a man is pictured holding one child, with two others next to him. The yellow star of David is visible on the small boy's coat. The picture of the Holocaust is startling as you read the Beatitudes. The concluding blessing about others who persecute you or speak badly about you is underneath a picture of Dr. Martin Luther King Jr. behind jail bars. Using this storybook with older children or youth would be a way to help them revisit this text in new ways, hearing and seeing new possibilities for the ways Jesus calls us to live.

Being at Home with the Bible

Biblical scholars talk about "texts of terror," those that we wish were not in the Bible because they are so difficult to understand, and we wonder, What kind of God would ask a father to sacrifice his son, send a flood to drown the world except for one family and a few pairs of animals? What kind of book is the Bible that it includes stories of rape and affairs, killing in God's name? What kind of book is the Bible that it tells women that they can't be leaders in the church, that they have to be silent? What kind of book is the Bible that it dares to suggest we should love all people and that the only thing that is required of us is to do justice, love kindness, and walk with God? What kind of book is the Bible that asks, Who is your neighbor? What kind of book is the Bible that says unless we share what we have, unless we care for others, unless we help the poor and visit those in prison, then we have not known or seen Jesus? It's all there in the Bible. We can't resolve the paradoxes that we read there. We are left to try and understand them both from the point of view of the original audience for whom they were written and from our modern-day perspective.

WITH THOUGHTFUL AND INTENTIONAL ENGAGEMENT WITH BIBLICAL STORIES, CHILDREN WILL GROW UP KNOWING THE BIBLE NOT AS A STRANGER OR GUEST BUT WILL BE AT HOME READING, WRESTLING, AND INTERPRETING STORIES FOR THEIR LIFE OF FAITH.

This chapter has only examined a few of the stories that are included in children's Bible storybooks. Hopefully it has provided you with some suggestions for helping parents and children hear and interpret ancient stories in new ways. In this way, a children's spiritual repertoire becomes rich and full. As Susan Burt reminds us, "Without encouragement to wander around the story, to wonder, to pull back the layers and look, children can be led on a straight and narrow, and soul-stifling path. But stories are not straight and narrow paths."[51]

Hymn writer Isaac Watts concluded his hymn version of the Twenty-Third Psalm with the line, "No more a stranger or a guest but like a child at home."[52] With thoughtful and intentional engagement with biblical stories, children will grow up knowing the Bible not as a stranger or guest but will be at home reading, wrestling, and interpreting stories for their life of faith.

- We become at home with the Bible when it becomes something more than a book on a shelf.

- We become at home with the Bible when we dare to open it and read with a child and pause for comments and questions.

- We become at home with the Bible when we are able to ask wondering questions and in so doing model how we read and hear an ancient story in a contemporary world.

- We become at home with the Bible when we seek to make

connections with old stories and new stories of our lives, lived in response to God's love and presence with us.

- We become at home with the Bible when we are able to dig deeper in it and remember it's not a book that will break apart, it will only break open.

How We Support Families with Children

How children's Bibles represent Jesus influences how their target readers perceive him. Children's Bibles driven by a particular set of concerns may form the child reader around those concerns, but in the end it is the concerns that dominate this formation. The child may, for instance, learn what she or he is to believe about Jesus, without ever entering the world of Jesus. Only those children's Bibles that seek to empower child readers, rather than to form them, will enable their readers to imagine the biblical world, reimagine the world they live in, and visualize Jesus for themselves.

—Melody Briggs

This final chapter turns to the practical with suggestions for workshops and conversations that churches can offer for parents and families. Forming children in the life of the Christian faith is the wonderful work of congregations and families. We do a good job of this formational and empowering work in congregational educational programs—church school, choir, mission, worship, VBS. But we don't always do a great job of educating parents for their part in partnering for the growth in faith of children. Faithful practices with the Bible begin at home. It's there where children are empowered to "imagine the biblical world" and make connections between this world and the world in which they are living. It's our job, no, it's our ministry as pastors and educators and church leaders, to support parents and other adult family members in this work of formation and empowerment.

Let's stop assuming that parents know what to do or where and how to begin.

LET'S STOP GIVING OUT BIBLES TO CHILDREN UNLESS WE ALSO START HELPING PARENTS LEARN WAYS TO BE INVOLVED IN READING WITH THEIR CHILD.

Let's stop waiting for parents to come to us asking for help, because it might be a long wait. Let's start by inviting parents to the table of conversation about how the Bible can be an important part of their continuing growth in the life of the Christian faith and also with their child or children. Let's stop giving out Bibles to children unless we also start helping parents learn ways to be involved in reading with their child. Let's stop assuming that everything a child needs to know and learn about faithful practices begins and ends in congregational educational programs. Let's start expecting parents to make their own commitments to involvement with their child's spiritual life.

Workshops or Conversations for Parents

In this chapter you will find ideas for workshops or conversations that your church can offer. They can be offered as a one-time event or in a series. They are designed for one-hour settings but could easily be adapted for a time frame that works best for your church.

1. How to Choose a Bible Storybook

Parents and grandparents could really use help with criteria to consider when buying a storybook. Whether you are shopping in an online bookstore or browsing through a bookstore or other retail store, it's helpful to provide family members with some things to consider before purchasing a storybook for reading with a child. Chapter 3 reviews a variety of storybooks and one children's Bible. Criteria for evaluation are also included. You could use information in that chapter for a 45- to 60-minute conversation. Here is a suggested design for the session.

Preparation: Order copies of at least two storybooks, one for younger children and one for older children. You could make these available for purchase at the end of the conversation. I would recommend the following: *Candle Read and Share, Bible Story Animals, Children of God Storybook Bible, Family Story Bible, Shine On: A Story Bible, Lion Read and Know.*

- 15 minutes—Overview of Bible storybooks, criteria to use in selection
- 15 minutes—Hands on with storybooks—have them available for parents to look at using the criteria
- 15 minutes—Discussion of what they saw, liked, would like to read with their child.

2. Conversations about the Bible

You realize that children who participate in your church's Christian education programs are learning a lot of Bible stories and are asking really good questions. You also realize that they may know more than their parents. You have decided to offer a series of conversations during the church school hour that focus on a variety of topics related to reading the Bible.

Revisiting the Bible

Use the concepts from chapter 1, remove, rearrange, and declutter to help parents identify their own experiences and issues in reading the Bible for themselves. This would be a great time to review assumptions about the Bible, what it is and what it is not.

What Gets in the Way of Reading the Bible with Your Child?

Use the information about fears of reading the Bible from chapter 2. A good way to begin would be to pass out index cards and ask parents to respond to these questions:

I would like to begin reading the Bible with my child but...

Is it an issue of:

- How and where to begin?
- Time?
- Knowledge and experience—what I do and don't know?
- Which storybook to use?
- Other?

What Your Child Is Learning about the Bible in Church School

Review the scope and sequence of the curriculum you are using for preschool and elementary-age children. Show where and how these same stories are told in selected children's Bible storybooks.

Questions about the Bible—from Children and Adults

As we know, children are often bold in their questions about the Bible. They are not shy about asking questions about miracles and healing, floods and seven days of creation. Adults probably have the same questions but are afraid to verbalize them. This session could feature an experienced church school teacher sharing some of the questions articulated by children. Parents could be invited to submit their questions on index cards, and this session or a follow-up session could focus on responses to the questions.

Reading the Bible with Your Child

Show several Bible storybooks like *Candle, Family Story Bible,* and *Shine On* and provide practical suggestions on how to begin.

3. The Bibles We Give

Many churches have the practice of giving a Bible to rising second or third graders. On the Sunday when they will be given, focus the church school session on that, providing guidance for the children and parents.

A first decision to be made is what to give. The best Bible is the *Deep Blue Kids Bible.* The good news about this Bible is that it is a complete Bible with notes appropriate for children. The down side is that it doesn't have many illustrations. Another option would be to give a really good storybook such as *Shine On* or *The Family Story Bible. Shine On* (Mennonite), *Spark Story Bible* (Evangelical Lutheran Church of America), and *Deep Blue Kids Bible* (United Methodist) are all designed to be used with children's church school curriculum.

Have the Bibles or Bible storybooks there for hands-on use. Play a scavenger hunt game with parents and children taking turns finding answers to these questions:

- Where is the story of Creation?
- Where can you find stories of Jesus's birth?
- Where in your Bible or Bible storybook is there information for parents?
- Find a picture about a story that is not familiar to you.
- Find a picture and a story that is very familiar to you.
- Find your favorite story. Why do you like it?

4. Conversations for Adults Who Are Waiting for the Adoption or Birth of a Child

Parents who are waiting to meet their child prepare in so many ways—like getting all the stuff required for a baby—bed, car seat, stroller. Nurses, doctors, and adoption counselors prepare parents for the delivery or receiving of the child and what to expect. Oftentimes the church is missing in these kinds of preparation activities. These conversations will focus on the topic of first steps in raising a child in the life of the Christian faith by reading Bible stories.

Here are some suggestions for conversation topics:

Experience with the Bible

Invite conversation about their experience with the Bible, both as a child growing up and now. These questions can help focus the conversation:

- What spiritual practices did you grow up with (prayer at meals or bedtime, reading the Bible, reading a Bible story-book, acts of service, seasonal celebrations such as an Advent wreath or Lenten practices, attending church school and worship)?
- As you think about introducing your child to the Christian faith through concrete practices at home, what are your hopes? Fears?
- When you think about reading the Bible with your child, what questions, concerns, or hopes do you have?
- What practices would you like to begin with?

Bible Storybook Options

Have several storybooks available for participants to look at. You could invite them to look at them using the criteria for review that are included in chapter 3. Focus on which ones work best for younger children.

Wondering with Children

Introduce the wondering approach to the participants by modeling it with them using the steps described in chapter 2: Enter, Hear, Pause, Wonder, and Bless.

5. Reading the Bible with Children: Telling a Bible Story

Chapter 1 provides information about the different ways that Bible stories are told. This book has been written to help support parents in taking a big step in getting started reading the Bible with their children. Bible stories are accessible through books and through storytellers on YouTube. There is a very old skill that some parents might be interested in learning—the skill of telling a Bible story.

In her chapter "Nurturing and Imaginative, Inquiring Spirit" in *Faith Forward,* Susan Burt offers some very practical suggestions for learning how to tell a story. It would be interesting to offer a workshop for parents who would like to learn this skill. If there is interest in your church, parents might also enjoy continuing as a group, learning and telling new stories that connect with the Bible stories that children are hearing and engaging with in the church school.

- Prepare by reading the text out loud. As you read, notice the setting where the story takes place, who the characters are, any information that is important to the story and that will help you remember as you tell it. Also notice what precedes and follows the story. After you read it, think about the meaning of the text. Does it have a "center of gravity," a main point?[1]

- Wonder about the text. Think about the characters in the story. Whose voices do you hear? Who is silent? What do you think the characters are feeling or thinking? Are there any details of the story that seem to be missing? Burt suggests, "Move about in the gaps, the spaces between the words, in the silences, and bring questions and wonderings to the text. . . . What questions arise when considering 'the other'—people of differing backgrounds, cultures, socioeconomic statuses, abilities, ages, stages, orientations."[2]

- Consider the children who are hearing the story—how will they engage the story? In what ways does it relate to their lives and their interests and abilities? How can you tell the story so children can engage it with all of their senses?

6. Reading Bible Stories and Connecting with Language Arts Skills That Children Are Learning in Elementary School

One of the most obvious and accessible ways we can support parents in reading the Bible with their children is to help them make connections between abilities children are learning in school and how these skills can be used in reading and interpreting the Bible.

For example, it is easy to access language arts curriculum maps for elementary age classes. One of the standards I examined was focused on the student's ability to read and comprehend a variety of literary texts. The indicators of their ability are described as: identify the main idea; analyze to determine first-person point of view; identify different kinds of figurative language (simile, metaphor, personification, and hyperbole); analyze the relationship among characters, setting, and plot in a text; analyze an author's craft, such as word structure; identify different kinds of writing. These same indicators are used at each grade level but with different instructional activities.

THE LITERARY SKILLS THAT A CHILD IS LEARNING ARE TRANSFERABLE IN HELPING A CHILD READ THE BIBLE.

If parents are tuned in to curriculum maps for their child's learning, then they are also aware of how they are learning to analyze texts and understand how an author communicates a story. The literary skills that a child is learning are transferable in helping a child read the Bible. Consider engaging parents in trying some of these methods with Bible stories their children are hearing and responding to in church school. All that is needed is for churches to let parents know the scope and sequence of stories for the year. It could be easily printed on a page to be posted with a magnet on the fridge.

These activities would be great for dinner table discussions:

Flat and Round Characters

Round characters are like real people you know. There is depth to them. We see them experience all of the realities of life. Sometimes they surprise us. Flat characters are ones that are more hidden. Very little is revealed or known about the character. There are no surprises.

Read the story of Miriam in Exodus 2:1-10 or Hagar in Genesis 21:1-21. Which characters are round, which are flat?

Venn Diagram

This exercise would be a great one to use in comparing Gospel accounts of a particular story like the birth of Jesus, feeding of the five thousand, or the woman who touched Jesus's clothes, or any story that is told in two Gospels. This would also work for the two stories of creation in Genesis 1 and 2.

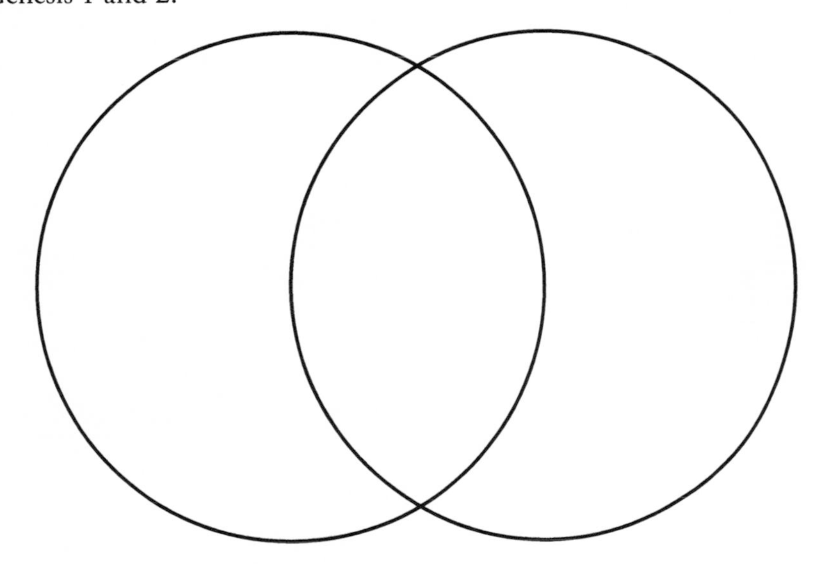

Draw two overlapping circles on a piece of paper. In the outer circles tell how the stories are different. In the inner circle where they overlap, tell how the stories are similar. This kind of exercise can lead children and adults into a discussion about different authors and different perspectives on events. Biblical scholars call this literary criticism. Children who are learning linguistic literary skills in school can use these same abilities with biblical text. A conversation such as this one invites all ages into wondering about stories in new ways.

Roundtable Discussion

Pick a Bible story for the week, perhaps one a child is studying in church school. With this kind of discussion, each person has a chance to say something about the story—what is intriguing, confusing, what they wonder about, what they would like to know more about. To make it easy, you could have a bowl on the dining table with titles of stories from the Bible written on slips of paper. If you want to be creative, you could write the story title and reference on a piece of paper and fold it into a paper fortune cookie (directions can easily be found on the web). Another fun presentation is to write the story title and text on a strip of paper and fold it into an origami star.

Finding Holes

This is a fun activity that only requires that you have a Bible storybook in front of you. Hearing the story and looking at the pictures, find a hole in the story where one of the characters disappears for a while, goes off camera, so to speak. Imagine what the character is doing when we can't see or hear him or her.[3] This would work well with many stories, such as Jesus visiting Mary and Martha or Jesus in the temple when he was a child.

What's Next

As we know, Bible stories we read are sometimes spare with details. A story is told and we are left wondering what happened to the character next. What happened to the Ethiopian official after he met Philip on the road? Or what do you think Zaccheus did after Jesus left his house? This kind of imagining about the story invites a child to stay with the story and think about implications. Or a child could be invited to put herself in the character of Mary, Jesus's mother, and think about what she did after Jesus left home.

Supporting Parents by Helping Them Read the Bible with Their Children

We give a card or a baptismal candle to a family at a child's baptism. What if we gave them a Bible storybook and a small booklet with suggestions about how to begin? Many churches have a practice of giving a Bible to children at second or third grade and again at either confirmation or high school graduation. I think we miss an opportunity by not giving or recommending a Bible storybook when a child is either dedicated or baptized in the congregation.

Chapter 3 reviews a variety of children's Bible storybooks. Two that would make great gifts are: *Candle Read and Share Bible* or the *Children of God, Storybook Bible*. If your church doesn't have the financial resources to give a storybook Bible, you could give a small booklet that would include a recommended list.

7. Give Laminate Bookmarks or Cards about Reading the Bible with a Child

Consider designing a booklet or laminate a bookmark or card that would include the following information:

Reading the Bible with Your Child—When and How to Begin

Bedtime is a great moment to begin a practice of closing the day with a story from the Bible and a prayer. Young children could listen to a short story. And most love to hear stories read or told to them by loving family members. Having a Bible storybook to read with a child at night, or even during the day, is a first step in forming a child in the life of the Christian faith.

Choosing a Bible Storybook

1. *The Children's Everyday Bible* (New York: DK Publishing, 2001) includes one story for every day of the year, 193 from the Old Testament and 172 from the New Testament.
2. *Children of God, Storybook Bible* (Grand Rapids: Zonderkidz, 2010).

3. *Candle Read and Share Bible* (UK: Thomas Nelson, 2007) includes 208 "bite-size stories."
4. *The Family Story Bible* (Louisville: Westminster John Knox Press, 1996) includes 58 stories from the Old Testament and 67 from the New Testament.
5. *Bible Animal Stories for Bedtime* (Barbour Publishing, 2011) includes 39 stories from the Old Testament and 22 from the New Testament. Each story includes a simple prayer.

Things to Remember

Introduce the story. If it's from the Old Testament, tell your child this is a story about a person who lived or something that happened a long time ago. If it's from the New Testament and it's a story about Jesus, you can tell your child that Jesus was God's Son who wanted God's people to learn how to love and live with others.

Wait for your child's questions or comments. Invite them to wonder about the story and the characters in it. As they grow older and are able to ask questions and make connections (around ages two to three) help them name the ways God wants them to live in the world.

8. Practices with the Bible at Home

It's helpful to provide parents with simple ideas for beginning a practice of reading the Bible with their child. How you communicate these ideas relates to what works best in your context. You could:

- Make these ideas available in a series of short articles in the church newsletter.
- Feature one of them a month in a blog for parents.
- Provide a simple handout that is given out at church school. The handout provides information for a month about the stories the child is hearing and learning in church school. Each story and text is listed with wondering questions for

a parent to use as she or he reads the story with their child. You could also include practical suggestions for how the parents can connect the biblical story with living the faith.

Other suggestions for Bible reading practices at home include:

Dinner Table Conversations

Offer suggestions for how families could engage a biblical story—perhaps one story a week. Include ideas for both a particular story and a process from ideas above: round and flat characters, round table discussion, Venn diagram, or finding holes.

Another simple way to engage Bible stories is to use the *God's Big Story Cards* from Faith Alive Resources (www.faithaliveresources.org). This small box of 165 cards has six suggestions for engaging with each story in imaginative ways—a great discussion starter at the table. Cost is $14.99.

Following Church Seasons

For the parent who wants to begin a spiritual practice with the Bible at home but doesn't know where or how to begin, following the seasons of the Christian calendar is a great way to start. To make it even easier, have a workshop after worship the week before a new season begins, where families learn about the season and make items to use during the season.

Another way to make it easy for families to start a spiritual practice would be to get a group of people together—teenagers, young adults, middle-aged, and older adults—to make seasonal bags for families to take home. All it takes is gathering together the necessary supplies and inviting people to come put the bags together. Canvas bags can be bought at craft stores or ordered online. Or fabric bags can be made using holiday cloth related to the church season. Bags can be made for checkout and returned, or they can be given to families. If you prefer to have them available for checkout and return, include a story Bible in the bag.

Be sure to place in each bag a laminated card that includes a simple introduction to each season, noting when it's celebrated and for how long, the color of the season and how it relates to the biblical stories, what's important about the season. Also helpful to include on this card are references to biblical texts that can be read during the season.

Advent – Purple or Royal Blue

- Include a table runner in the color of the season, either purple or royal blue. There are probably several people in the congregation who would like to contribute their time and sewing machine to stitching a simple runner or rectangle table topper.
- Include directions for making an advent wreath to use during the four weeks leading up to Christmas. Also provide a very simple advent liturgy that families could use at the dinner table.
- Create an Advent Calendar in a Jar. Download the free instructions for this activity at home from the Mustard Seed Website (http://msainfo.us/2012/12/11/advent-in-a-jar/).
- Create an advent chain. Provide strips of paper with an activity or reading, one on each strip. Children can open one strip each day before Christmas. The web has a variety of different information to include. The Patheos website includes a different biblical text and symbol for each day. (See patheos.com – Advent chains for directions.)
- Make a Jesse tree. This is a reference to the Isaiah 11:1 text about Jesus being born in the family line of Jesse. A Jesse tree can be a branch decorated with paper symbols that represent all the people and events leading up to the birth of Jesus. Instructions for making a Jesse tree are available from the website of the Reformed Church of America (www.rca.org/resources/jesse-tree-family-devotions).

Lent—Purple

- Include a table runner in the color or the season, which is purple. There are probably several people in the congregation who would like to contribute their time and sewing machine to stitching a simple runner or rectangle table topper.

1. Include a handout with ideas for family observation of Lent. There are several resources that could be downloaded and printed to include in the Lenten bag. Check out these websites:
    a. Mustard Seed Associates have a website that provides a link to a wide variety of resources for Lent and Easter. (http://godspace-msa.com/2014/02/19/resources-for-celebrating-lent-for-kids-2014/).
2. One-page handout—Sharing Lent with children, 7 tips for Making Lent Meaningful: Give up/take up, slow down, read, commit, be kind, volunteer, and donate (http://kidsfriendly.org.nz/wp-content/Uploads/Sharing-Lent-with-Children2.pdf).

- Bake during Lent and make pretzels together. Pretzels are a simple Lenten symbol of arms in prayer. Simple recipes for children are available on the web (for example, http://www.grit.com/community/pretzels-the-official-bread-of-lent.aspx).

Holy Week

- Make Holy Week boxes at home. This simple box helps children recall and retell the events of Holy Week from Palm Sunday to Easter. Directions are available at this blog: https://camillelebronpowell.wordpress.com/2013/03/18/.

Easter—White

- Include a table runner in the color or the season, which is white. There are probably several people in the congregation who would like to contribute their time and sewing machine to stitching a simple runner or rectangle table topper.

- Empty Tomb Biscuits are a fun and easy thing to make with children as you tell or read the Easter story. Recipes are plentiful. Here's one link: http://www.celebratingholidays.com/?page_id=3282.

Pentecost—Red

Pentecost is celebrated as the birthday of the church when we remember the gift of God's Spirit to the church, as told in Acts 2:1-31.

- Include a table runner in the color or the season, which is red. There are probably several people in the congregation who would like to contribute their time and sewing machine to stitching a simple runner or rectangle table topper. To save time, you could make the runners or table toppers with different colors on top and bottom so they can be used for at least two different seasons.
- A great resource for craft ideas, baking, and games that can be played at home to celebrate Pentecost is available free at http://kidsfriendly.org.nz/wp-content/Uploads/Celebrating-Pentecost-2015.pdf

Ordinary Time—Green

The longest season of the church calendar follows the celebration of Pentecost. It is known as Ordinary Time, and it lasts until the first Sunday of Advent, which occurs in either late November or the first Sunday in December. One of the ways to help families stay connected with spiritual practices is to provide things in this bag that they can use on Sundays when they might be out of town or not able to participate in church school and worship. You could fill this bag with a variety of items for families to use: suggestions for Bible stories to read for Sundays in June and July; crossword puzzles and other kinds of games using Bible stories. Look at this website for additional ideas to include: www.vibrantfaithathome.org/.

9. Coffee, Tea, and Conversation

I have a friend, Carol Wehrheirm, who loves to teach sixth graders. She taught this age group for fourteen years in her church. She is also an experienced curriculum writer, editor, and children's author, and her hands-on experience has been invaluable to her work. A year ago some mothers approached her about what their children were learning in church school. They admitted that their children knew more about the Bible than they did and they wanted some help. So they asked Carol if she would meet with them on Wednesday afternoons while their children were in choir practice. She agreed and this small group of moms and dads began to meet together every week during the church school year.

Carol uses a very simple format for her forty-five-minute conversation with such parents. The passage is read out loud and then they discuss the text, responding to several questions about the text that Carol has prepared. Each text is then related to the faith of the parent and how it makes a difference in their life. In a short space of time, parents engage the same text their child will be hearing in church school. They are prepared and hopefully ready to engage the story at home as together they think about its meaning for their lives of faith. When might such an informal conversation work in your congregational context? If church school does not meet the same time as worship, this kind of conversation could take place then.

10. Bible Study Opportunities for Parents and Adults

What kinds of times and settings would work best for offering Bible study options for parents? Denominational publishing houses produce a variety of curricular resources for adults who want to engage in Bible study. A great overview of how to lead studies is the book *Teaching Biblical Faith, Leading Small Group Bible Studies* by Jack Seymour (Abingdon Press, 2015). A variety of approaches that can be used with small-group studies are explained in this most helpful book. Perhaps there is an adult in the congregation who would be interested in working with a pastor or educator and teach a group of young adult parents.

Another excellent resource for basic Bible study is *Covenant*, the newest adult discipleship curriculum available from The United Methodist Publishing House. This study is designed for one and a half hour sessions and includes a leader and participant guide, as well as DVD presentations by biblical scholars.

For those who want to learn more about the Bible by participation in a DVD study, consider using *Opening Doors to Discipleship, Education and Faith Formation*. The courses on *Teaching Skills* and *Bible Background* would be especially helpful. You can learn more about this program which has been created and sponsored by the Presbyterian Reformed Educational Partners at www.odtd.net.

Getting Close

Chapter 1 began with a wonderful quote from Rabbi Sandy Sasso who is a creative children's author. She tells us that good stories remind us of who we are and what we believe. She is correct! Engaging good stories in the Bible also provides us with the opportunity to reflect on how these stories relate to our beliefs and how those beliefs are lived and acted in the world.

The news we read and hear every day reminds us of the importance of being involved in the lives of our children. With the myriad of choices available to them in the culture, the intention of our spiritual practices becomes even more important as we help nurture the development of their face of faith for seeing and acting in the world.

ENGAGING GOOD STORIES IN THE BIBLE ALSO PROVIDES US WITH THE OPPORTUNITY TO REFLECT ON HOW THESE STORIES RELATE TO OUR BELIEFS AND HOW THOSE BELIEFS ARE LIVED AND ACTED IN THE WORLD.

Charles was adopted into a faithful family who is involved in many of the educational activities of their church. Charles has always seemed to be a child who was interested in spiritual questions. Two years ago, his mother received the following e-mail, which had been passed on from his teacher. The mother of a special needs child in his kindergarten class wanted to share the story with Charles's mother.

> I was walking James into school this morning and he was stopping a lot, not excited about going to school. (Imagine that?!) I could tell a "melt down" was coming, when a little boy came up beside James and put his arm around him. He said, "Come on, James, I will help you." Immediately James starts walking. As the two of them are walking into the school, the little boy says to me, "My name is Charles and James listens to me... because I am the voice on his learning device." (James has a device at school where he can push a button to say what he wants—no, yes, outside, more, etc. and they've used Charles's voice to be James's voice!) I said, "Wow, thank you so much, Charles. How old are you?" Charles says, "I am six and three quarters!" They continue to walk, Charles keeps his arm around James's shoulder the whole time. At one point, he stops to adjust James's backpack which is slipping off. As I fought back the tears, we arrive inside the building to the point where I must let James walk alone. I ask him for a kiss, which he gives me—mouth fully open. Then Charles, who hasn't taken his arm off of James this whole time, looks straight at me and says, "Don't worry, I'll take care of him," and together, arm in arm, James and Charles walked to their classroom. It was then I realized that THAT is what life is about on so many levels. Taking care of people. Watching out for one another. Loving unconditionally. It's moments like that that keep special needs parents like myself encouraged and hopeful! This is cause for a HUGE celebration.... I'm thinking Ben & Jerry's ice cream for breakfast!!
>
> P.S. Turns out Charles kept his word all day!! Got this photo this afternoon where he was spending time with James in free play.

The photo shows two smiling children, arms around each other. When I think about the story of the Good Samaritan, which we looked at in chapter 4, I think of this story of James and Charles. Charles was not just James's voice on his learning device, Charles was his friend. He hung around with him to help him, to make sure he would be okay, and that he would have a friend. I know Charles has probably heard the story of the Good Samaritan in church school, and in times with the children in worship. Maybe he also is beginning to interpret the story and its meaning for how he lives faithfully in the world.

And then there is James. He reminds me of the man whom the Good Samaritan helped. We never hear the voice of the injured man. It's interesting to wonder about what he was thinking about the incident. I wonder how James will remember stories of those who responded to him and his disability. I hope both sets of parents will keep this story for their sons and help them remember how getting close to the biblical text with our lives makes a difference, for us and for others.

In the quote at the beginning of this chapter, Melody Briggs suggests the importance of the role of children's Bible storybooks in moving beyond formation to empowering readers to enter the world of Jesus and to imagine how that ancient world has relationship with the contemporary world. Both are necessary, I think. We need to make commitments to supporting parents in formational Christian practices of reading and engaging biblical texts. In doing so, we enable parents and children to be empowered to live faithfully in response to these stories of God's love for all humankind. Thanks be to God for the power and promise of these stories.

A Wondering Model of Questions

This model of questions can be used with children at home. Try reading a Bible story together from one of the Bible storybooks recommended in this book, and engage the stories using these simple steps. This is a great way to help a child close down his or her day.

Enter

Find that place where you will read together. It may be a comfortable chair or it may be the child's bedroom with you sitting next to him or her. As you begin to help a child make the transition from playtime or bath time or from doing homework to this special time, questions like these can help with the transition:

- How was your day today?
- Was there something that made you really laugh?
- Was there something that made you sad?

The *Examen* is an ancient spiritual practice of examining the day before going to sleep. The *Examen* asks you to be aware of God's presence as you review the day.

- Where did you see God's love today?
- Where did you give or receive God's love? For what are you most grateful?
- For what are you least grateful?

Hear

Reading the story together can be done several ways. You can simply follow in order the stories that are included in the storybook you are using. You could be familiar with the stories that are being used in your child's church school class and be sure to read that one in the week preceding and following the Sunday it is used.

Pause

Pausing means we take a few seconds, maybe a minute, just to sit with the story in silence. Of course, this is not so easy with young children. But the practice can grow with them. With a three-year-old, you could count to ten silently with fingers, and when you have counted all ten, then it's time to move to wondering questions.

Wonder

This part of the model invites the child to explore the story. Simpler questions are best with younger children; some questions that can be used to help a child engage and reflect on the story are these:

1. Who is in the story and what happens to them?

This is a great question for all ages, especially young children. With this basic question, children are introduced to a tool of literary analysis that seeks to identify in each story the characters, the setting, and the plot. Older children are, of course, able to identify the plot more so than younger children. As they respond to the question about who is in the story, other questions you could use are *Why* questions (Why do you think Jonah ran away?) and/or *What if* questions (What if Jonah had said yes to God rather than no?).

2. What do you think this story is about?

If the story is one that Jesus told, you could ask, "Why do you think Jesus told this story?" This is a good open-ended question because it invites the hearer to respond with his or her own interpretation. Just imagine how a child's answer to this question could change as he or she grows older.

3. What kind of story is this?

This question is more appropriate for older children who are reading on their own and know about different kinds of writing.

4. How is this story different from the time and place in which we live?

This question works best for older children. It invites them to wonder about the time and culture and the original audience for which the story was written. This kind of thinking encourages a child to think about the text from a historical point of view, a kind of biblical analysis that scholars have been using for a long time. It also provides a beginning step in cultural analysis, understanding the story and its meaning for the reader who hears it in a very different time and place. Inviting a child to notice the artwork accompanying the story is a good way to engage this question too.

5. Why do you think this story is important?

This kind of question asks a child for his or her own analysis of the story. With younger children you could ask, "Do you like this story? Why or why not?"

6. How do you connect with the story or what does this story have to do with your life? Or, When would be a good time to remember this story?

Bless

As you end this practice of reading the Bible together, select one or more of the following that work for you:

- Affirm some of the things you have heard the child say about the story.
- Recall some of the good things or bad things mentioned by the child at the beginning and use them in a simple prayer of thanks or a prayer for help.
- Invite the child to pray. This could help him or her learn how to use different kinds of prayers: thanksgiving, intercession, confession, and praise.

APPENDIX 2

Evaluating Children's Bible Storybooks

1. Content

- Which books/stories are included/omitted? Why?
- How many Old Testament and New Testament stories are present?
- How is the story told? Are text references included? Does it invite wonder? Does it fill in gaps in the story? Does it conflate or harmonize texts? (For example, does it tell the birth story of Jesus by putting together the stories from Matthew and Luke rather than telling the story with the differences in the two Gospels.)
- What translation of the Bible is the story based on?
- Are the stories from the Old Testament allowed to stand on their own without being connected to stories of Jesus?
- Is inclusive language for God used?

2. Organization, ease of use for parents and children, resources, index

- Is there an introduction for parents or children?
- Is the biblical citation given for the stories?
- Is there any kind of introduction to the two testaments and to the different kinds of writing in each?
- What additional resources, if any, does this Bible storybook have?
- Is there an index of stories or table of contents?

3. Layout and appropriateness for reader—what helps the child understand and interpret the story for his or her life? Are there questions that invite the child to engage the story?

4. Art

- What kind of art is used to illustrate the stories—realistic, contemporary, child-friendly?
- In what ways do the illustrations contribute to the story?

Appendix 3

Bible Storybooks for Children—A Recommended List

Easing Children into the Bible: Preschool Two to Six

1. *The Children's Everyday Bible*

This book (New York: DK Publishing, 2001) includes one story for every day of the year, 193 from the Old Testament and 172 from the New Testament.

2. *The International Children's Story Bible*

This book (Thomas Nelson, 1993) by Mary Hollingsworth selects 105 stories that represent diversity in the kinds of writing found in the Bible: history, wisdom literature, Gospels, and letters. Stories are chosen for their accessibility to younger children. Each story is one page with an accompanying illustration drawn by a child.

3. *Children of God Storybook Bible*

This book (Grand Rapids: Zonderkidz, 2010) by Archbishop Desmond Tutu shares a similar commitment to helping children begin to read the Bible from a multicultural perspective. The fifty-six stories are chosen to show the ways that God works through history and how God wants all people to love each other. In their commitment to designing a global children's Bible, the stories are illustrated by artists from around the world. Each story is on two pages and ends with a prayer.

4. Candle Read and Share Bible

This book (United Kingdom: Thomas Nelson, 2007) includes 208 "bite-size Stories," some from books that are often omitted from children's Bible storybooks: Esther, Job, Ecclesiastes, and Isaiah. Each story includes the biblical citation and a comment or a question for the child to consider. The illustrations are bright and colorfully drawn in a character (cartoon style) that works well with young children.

5. The Family Story Bible and *The Lectionary Story Bible*

The Family Story Bible (Louisville: Westminster John Knox Press, 1996) includes fifty-eight stories from the Old Testament and sixty-seven from the New Testament. As young children improve with their reading skills, *The Family Story Bible* and *The Lectionary Story Bible* can become important storybooks for introductions to many treasured stories in the Bible. Ralph Milton provides an excellent selection of favorite stories of women and men in a contemporary storytelling format including many illustrations. Then Milton expanded this work into three volumes, *The Lectionary Story Bible*, Year A (2007), B (2008), and C (2009) (Kelowna, BC Canada: Woodlake Books). All three volumes use inclusive language for God, and the illustrations of Margaret Kyle invite the reader or hearer into the story, thus making this book accessible to nonreaders.

6. Bible Animal Stories for Bedtime

This title by Jane Landreth (Uhrichsville, OH: Barbour Publishing, 2011) organizes its collection of stories by animals. This is a small book and each story is told on three pages and concludes with a prayer. This would be a great beginning storybook for younger children.

Younger Elementary-Age Children: Ages Six to Eight

1. The Lion Read and Know Bible

This book (United Kingdom: Lion Children's Books, 2008) includes twenty-five stories from the Old Testament and twenty-four from the New Testament. Though this is a small collection of stories, they are representative of the major characters of the Old Testament and the variety of kinds of stories included about Jesus in the Gospel portion of the New Testament: birth, teachings, parables, healing stories, death, and resurrection. The story of Pentecost, one story of Paul, and the book of Revelation is all that is included for the rest of the New Testament.

2. The Jesus Storybook Bible: Every Story Whispers His Name

This collection (Grand Rapids: Zondervan, 2007) has twenty-one stories from the Old Testament and twenty-three stories from the New Testament and is written by Sally Lloyd-Jones. This title is different from others in two ways. First, the author wants the child who is hearing or reading these stories to understand that the Bible is "telling one Big Story," which is the story of God's love and centers on the story of a baby, and this connection is made very explicitly. So the story of the birth of Isaac in Genesis concludes by connecting it to the birth of Jesus. The story of Jonah who spent three days inside the fish is connected to Jesus's death and resurrection. A parent who is reading this book with a child should be prepared to understand the connection Jones is making between the Old Testament story and the life of Jesus.

3. Shine On: A Story Bible

This book (Elgin, IL: Brethren Press, 2014) uses the New Revised Standard Version translation for the stories, with 146 from the Old Testament and 156 from the New Testament. There are two distinctives that make this storybook unique. Each story is presented on two pages. The illustration is given more room than the story, which invites the reader into the story in strong visual ways. The illustrations are varied in form and style because of the different artists whose work is included.

The second thing that makes this storybook stand out is the use of three questions designed to invite the reader to wonder and reflect on the story, explore it deeper in order to understand its meaning, and connect the story with his or her own life. In the introduction, the editors make it clear that they hope that their collection will be read and discussed in family settings at home and at the church.

4. The Bible for Children

This title (Intercourse, PA: Good Books, 2002) provides over two hundred stories retold for children.

Elementary-Age Children: Ages Nine to Eleven

1. Deep Blue Kid's Bible

This book (Nashville: Common English Bible, 2012) is a children's version of the newest Bible to be translated, the *Common English Bible.* Three children, Asia, Edgar, and Kat act as guides to help children dive into the Bible. In addition to an introduction to each book of the Bible, there are in-text notes that help children understand and begin to connect with difficult and challenging biblical texts. Other features include maps, Bible exploration tools and facts, challenges for reading and remembering, and ways to connect text and life.

2. The Children's Illustrated Bible

This book (New York: DK Publishing, 2005) has stories by Selina Hastings and illustrations by Eric Thomas and combines several biblical resources into one volume. It includes an introduction to the Bible; overviews of particular time periods, such as the patriarchs, life in Egypt, daily life in Jesus's time, and the early church; and maps and a list of people named in the stories. Each story also includes side bar information that provides historic and cultural information.

3. The CEB Student Bible

This title (Nashville: Common English Bible, 2015) is appropriate for middle school and older youth. It includes introductions to each book of the Bible written in language for teenagers. Articles, discussion questions, and prayers and reflections written by youth make this a great Bible for this age group.

Additional Bible Storybooks

1. The Pilgrim Book of Bible Stories

This storybook (Cleveland: Pilgrim Press, 2003) takes a very creative approach to the selection of included Bible stories. It is divided into nineteen chapters and includes stories from the laws of Leviticus, wisdom literature, and prophecy—the kinds of writings that are usually not included in children's Bibles.

2. JPS Illustrated Children's Bible

These stories (Philadelphia: Jewish Publication Society, 2009) are retold by Ellen Frankel. The illustrations by award-winning artist Avi Katz invite the reader into the drama and feelings of the stories.

3. The Read and Learn Bible

This Bible storybook published by the American Bible Society includes many stories, simply told with colorful illustrations. Most stories also include a brief textbox with information about some aspect of the story. This collection of stories would work well as a first storybook for young children.

4. *The Mystic Bible*

This title, published by Sophia Books in 2012, includes stories about Jesus from his birth through the Pentecost story. They are written by Alexandra Sangster in a poetry style that invites children to explore familiar stories through a new perspective.

5. *Bible Stories and Psalms for Young Children*

Psalms for Young Children (Grand Rapids, MI: Eerdmans Books for Young Readers, 2008) includes a collection of forty psalms retold for young readers by Marie Hélène Delval and illustrated by the artist Arno. This same author also has a very small collection of nine stories from the Bible, *The Bible for Young Children* (Grand Rapids, MI: Eerdmans Books for Young Readers, 2008). They are retold simply with beautiful illustrations.

6. *Five-Minute Bible Stories*

Lois Rock has retold twelve stories from the Old Testament and eight stories from the New Testament in *Five-Minute Bible Stories* (Minneapolis: Augsburg Fortress, 2005). Each story includes a very brief introduction and then tells the story with lovely illustrations by Richard Johnson.

7. *The Spark Story Bible*

This is a book (Minneapolis: Augsburg Fortress, 2009) designed to be used by children in a church school setting. It is the storybook that goes with the children's curriculum *Spark*. It includes forty-five stories from the Old Testament and 105 stories from the New Testament.

8. *Bible Storybooks*

Bible Storybooks by Rabbi Sandy Eisenberg Sasso should be included in church libraries for children. These books do a wonderful job of helping children connect biblical stories with life:

1. *Creation's First Light* (Indianapolis: IBJ Book Publishing, 2013)

2. *In God's Name* (Woodstock, VT: Jewish Lights Publishing, 2004)

3. *But God Remembered: Stories of Women from Creation to the Promised Land* (Woodstock, VT: Jewish Lights Publishing, 2008)

4. *God's Paintbrush* (Woodstock, VT: Jewish Lights Publishing, 2004)

5. *God In Between* (Woodstock, VT: Jewish Lights Publishing, 1998)

6. *Noah's Wife: The Story of Naamah* (Woodstock, VT: Jewish Lights Publishing, 2002)

7. *God Said Amen* (Woodstock, VT: Jewish Lights Publishing, 2000)

8. *Cain and Abel: Finding the Fruits of Peace* (Woodstock, VT: Jewish Lights Publishing, 2001)

9. *Adam and Eve's First Sunset: God's New Day* (Woodstock, VT: Jewish Lights Publishing, 2003)

10. *For Heaven's Sake* (Woodstock, VT: Jewish Lights Publishing, 1999)

Notes

Introduction

1. John Jacob Niles, *Songs of the Hill-Folk: Twelve Ballads from Kentucky, Virginia, and North Carolina* (New York: G. Schirmer, 1934), 9.

2. "America's Changing Religious Landscape," Pew Research Center's Religion and Public Life, May 12, 2015, http://www.pewforum.org/2015/05/12/americas-changing-religious-landscape/.

3. "'Nones' on the Rise," Pew Research Center's Religion and Public Life, October 9, 2012, http://www.pewforum.org/2012/10/09/nones-on-the-rise/.

4. Mark Chaves, *American Religion: Contemporary Trends* (Princeton: Princeton University Press, 2011), 37.

5. "The State of the Bible: 6 Trends for 2014," Barna Group, April 8, 2014, https://www.barna.org/barna-update/culture/664-the-state-of-the-bible-6-trends-for-2014#.VVoOtSFViko.

6. Parker Palmer, *The Courage to Teach: Exploring the Inner Landscape of a Teacher's Life* (San Francisco: Jossey-Bass: 2007), 116.

1. What Story Does the Bible Tell?

Epigraph: Sandy Eisenberg Sasso, "Tell Me a Story: Narrative and the Religious Imagination of Children," in *Faith Forward: Re-Imagining Children's and Youth Ministry*, vol. 2 (Canada: Wood Lake Books, 2015), 101.

1. Christian Smith with Melinda Lundquist Denton, *Soul Searching: The Religious and Spiritual Lives of American Teenagers* (New York: Oxford Press, 2005), 131–32.

2. Kenda Creasy Dean, *Almost Christian: What the Faith of Our Teenagers Is Telling the American Church* (New York: Oxford University Press: 2010), 19.

3. Smith with Denton, *Soul Searching,* 261.

4. Ibid., 262.

5. Krista Tippett, "The Spirituality of Parenting," *On Being* interview with Rabbi Sandy Sasso, June 17, 2010.

6. Dean, *Almost Christian,* 10–11.

7. James D. Smart, *The Strange Silence of the Bible in the Church: A Study in Hermeneutics* (Philadelphia: The Westminster Press, 1970), 168–69.

8. John Westerhoff, *Bringing Up Children in the Christian Faith* (San Francisco: Harper and Row, 1980), 37.

9. Daniel Aleshire, "Finding Eagles in the Turkeys' Nest: Pastoral Theology and Christian Education," *Review and Expositer* 85 (1988): 699.

10. Craig Dykstra, *Growing in the Life of Faith: Education and Christian Practices,* 2nd ed. (Louisville, KY: Westminster John Knox, 2005), 125–26.

11. Ibid., 155.

12. Dean, *Almost Christian,* 39.

13. *Shine On: A Story Bible* (Elgin, IL: Brethren Press, 2014), 5.

14. Archbishop Desmond Tutu, *Children of God Storybook Bible* (Grand Rapids, MI: Zondervan, 2010), 5.

15. Gwen Ellis, *Candle Read and Share Bible* (Oxford: Candle Books, 2007), vi.

16. Sally Lloyd-Jones, *The Jesus Storybook Bible: Every Story Whispers His Name* (Grand Rapids: Zonderkidz, 2007), 17.

17. Mark Water, *The Pilgrim Book of Bible Stories* (Cleveland: Pilgrim Press, 2003), 5.

18. *The Deep Blue Kids Bible* (Nashville: Common English Bible, 2012), 3.

19. Melody Briggs, "The Word Became Visual Text: The Boy Jesus in Children's Bibles," in *Text, Image & Otherness in Children's Bibles: What Is in the Picture?,* eds. Caroline Vander Stichele and Hugh S. Pyper (Atlanta: Society of Biblical Literature, 2012), 166.

20. Ellis, *Candle Read and Share Bible,* 289.

21. Sophie Piper, *The Lion Read and Know Bible* (Oxford: Lion Children's, 2008), 203.

22. Lloyd-Jones, *The Jesus Storybook Bible,* 169.

23. Briggs, "The Word Became Visual Text: The Boy Jesus in Children's Bibles," in *Text, Image & Otherness in Children's Bibles, What Is in the Picture?,* 153.

24. Ibid., 158.

25. Ibid.

26. Angie Smith, *For Such a Time as This: Stories of Women from the Bible Retold for Girls* (Nashville: B&H Publishing, 2014), 183.

27. Ibid., 184.

28. Ibid., 185.

29. Ibid.

30. Ralph Milton, *The Family Story Bible (*Louisville: Westminster John Knox Press, 1996), 223.

31. *Shine On: A Story Bible* (Elgin, IL: Brethren Press, 2014), 224–25.

32. Katherine Paterson, *The Invisible Child: On Reading and Writing Books for Children* (New York: Dutton Children's Books, 2001), 238, 239.

2. How Can We Use Children's Natural Curiosity to Help Them Read the Bible?

Epigraph: Susan Burt, "Nurturing an Imaginative, Inquiring Spirit" in *Faith Forward: A Dialogue on Children, Youth, and a New Kind of Christianity*, vol. 1, eds. David M. Csinos and Melvin Bray (Kelowna, BC: CopperHouse, 2013), 121–122.

1. These stages are clearly described in James Fowler, "The Public Church Ecology for Faith Education and Advocate for Children" in *Faith Development in Early Childhood*, ed. Doris A. Blazer (Kansas City: Sheed and Ward, 1989), 140.

2. T. Wyatt Watkins, "Unfettered Wonder: Rediscovering Prayer through the Voices of Children," in *Nurturing Children's Spirituality: Christian Perspectives and Best Practices*, ed. Holly Catterton Allen (Eugene, OR: Cascade Books, 2008), 137.

3. Jerome W. Berryman, *The Spiritual Guidance of Children* (New York: Morehouse Publishing, 2013), 1.

4. Kevin J. Swick, "Strengthening Families for the Task," in *Faith Development in Early Childhood*, ed. Doris A. Blazer (Kansas City: Sheed and Ward, 1989), 112.

5. Sandy Eisenberg Sasso, "Tell Me a Story: Narrative and the Religious Imagination of Children," in *Faith Forward: Re-Imagining Children's and Youth Ministry*, vol. 2, eds. David M. Csinos and Melvin Bray (Kelowna, BC: CopperHouse, 2015), 98–99.

6. Niles, *Songs of the Hill-Folk*, 9.

7. Jerome W. Berryman, *The Complete Guide to Godly Play*, vol. 8 (Denver: Morehouse Education Resources, 2012), 7.

8. Jerome W. Berryman, *Teaching Godly Play: How to Mentor the Spiritual Development of Children* (Denver: Morehouse Education Resources, 2009), 42.

9. The wondering questions remain the same with each story. Ibid., 49–50.

10. Marc Gellman and Thomas Hartman, *How Do You Spell God?* (New York: HarperTrophy, 1998), 145–146.

11. Mark Roncace, "Conflating Creation, Combining Christmas, and Ostracizing the Other," in *Text, Image and Otherness in Children's Bibles: What Is in the Picture?* eds. Caroline Vander Stichele and Hugh S. Pyper (Atlanta: Society of Biblical Literature, 2012), 205.

12. Theodore Hiebert, "The Tower of Babel and Biblical Community," in *APCE Advocate* (Winter 2007).

13. This concept is explained more fully in Rabbi Sandy Eisenberg Sasso, *Midrash: Reading the Bible with Question Marks* (Brewster, MA: Paraclete Press, 2013).

14. Roncace, "Conflating Creation, Combining Christmas, and Ostracizing the Other," in *Text, Image and Otherness in Children's Bibles, What Is in the Picture?*, 205.

15. Ellis, *Candle Read and Share Bible*, 337.

16. Desmond Tutu, *Children of God Storybook Bible* (Grand Rapids: Zonderkidz, 2010), 95.

17. Thanks to T. C. Anderson, a former student, and now pastor, who kept asking this question in class.

18. Timothy Beal, "Childrens' Bibles Hot and Cold," in *Text, Image and Otherness in Children's Bibles: What Is in the Picture?*, eds. Caroline Vander Stichele and Hugh S. Pyper (Atlanta: Society of Biblical Literature, 2012), 314.

19. Ibid., 315.

20. Ibid., 316.

21. Marc Gellman, *God's Mailbox: More Stories about Stories in the Bible* (New York: Morrow Junior Books, 1996), xii.

3. What Bibles and Bible Storybooks Do We Read with Children?

Epigraph: James Fowler, "The Public Church Ecology for Faith Education and Advocate for Children" in *Faith Development in Early Childhood,* ed. Doris A. Blazer (Kansas City: Sheed and Ward 1989), 147.

1. Sally Lloyd-Jones, *The Jesus Storybook Bible, Every Story Whispers His Name* (Grand Rapids: Zondervan, 2007), 17.

2. *Shine On: A Story Bible* (Elgin, IL: Brethren Press, 2014), 5.

3. *International Children's Story Bible* (Dallas: Word Publishing, 1990).

4. Murray Watts, *The Bible for Children* (Intercourse, PA: Good Books, 2002), 12.

5. Lois Rock, *Five-Minute Bible Stories* (Minneapolis: Augsburg Fortress, 2005), 56.

6. Ellen Frankel, *JPS Illustrated Children's Bible* (Philadelphia: Jewish Publication Society, 2009), xi.

7. Ibid., 227.

8. Water, *Pilgrim Book of Bible Stories,* 5.

9. Andrew Knowles, *The Crossroad Children's Bible* (New York: Crossroad Publishing, 1982).

10. Water, *The Pilgrim Book of Bible Stories,* 3.

11. Milton, *The Family Story Bible,* 7.

12. Sarah Hinlicky Wilson, "R-rated, How to Read the Bible with Children" in *The Christian Century* 130, no. 5 (February 25, 2013): 22.

13. Melanie Dennis Unrau, "Where Are the Girls in Children's Bibles?" *geez* (Spring, 2013): 43.

14. Ibid. The criteria of women who speak or act is included as a part of the Bechdel test, which is used by feminists in evaluating women's presence in film. The requirement is that the film needs to have at least two women in it who both talk with each other and in conversations speak about something other than a man.

15. *International Children's Story Bible,* n.p.

16. Milton, *Family Story Bible,* 8.

17. Murray Watts, *The Bible for Children,* 12.

18. Water, *The Pilgrim Book of Bible Stories,* 3.

19. Frankel, *JPS Illustrated Children's Bible,* xiii.

20. Ibid., 227.

21. Ibid., 233.

22. Sandy Eisenberg Sasso, *God's Echo: Exploring Scripture with Midrash* (Brewster, MA: Paraclete Press, 2007), 30.

23. Marie Héléne Delval, *Psalms for Young Children* (Grand Rapids, MI: Eerdmans Books for Young Readers, 2003).

24. *Spark Story Bible* (Minneapolis: Augsburg Fortress, 2009), 1.

25. Brendan Powell Smith, *The Brick Bible: A New Spin on the Old Testament* (New York: Skyhorse Publishing, 2011).

26. Milton, *Family Story Bible,* 8.

4. Stories That Form Us for a Life of Faith

Epigraph: T. Wyatt Watkins, "Unfettered Wonder: Rediscovering Prayer Through the Inspired Voices of Children," *Children's Spirituality, Christian Perspectives and Best Practices,* ed. Holly Catterton Allen (Eugene, OR: Cascade Books, 2008), 133.

1. Peter J. Gomes, *The Good Book* (New York: William Morrow and Company, 1996), 6.

2. Amy-Jill Levine, *Short Stories by Jesus: The Enigmatic Parables of a Controversial Rabbi* (New York: HarperOne, 2014), 275.

3. *Shine On: A Story Bible,* 5.

4. Frankel, *JPS Illustrated Children's Bible,* 233.

5. Watts, *The Bible for Children,* 22.

6. Ibid., 26.

7. Marie-Hèléne Delval, *The Bible for Young Children* (Grand Rapids: Eerdmans Books for Young Readers, 2002), 18.

8. Theodore Hiebert, note on Gen 7:12-24, *CEB Study Bible* (Nashville: CEB, 2013), 16.

9. *Story #11, God's Big Story,* (Grand Rapids: Faith Alive Christian Resources). See www.dwellcurriculum.org.

10. Ibid., Story #12.

11. Levine, *Short Stories by Jesus,* 37.

12. Lois Rock, *Five-Minute Bible Stories,* 82.

13. Selina Hastings, *Children's Illustrated Bible* (New York: DKPublishing, 1992), 238.

14. *Shine On: A Story Bible*, 230–31.

15. Levine, *Short Stories by Jesus,* 41.

16. *Deep Blue Kids Bible,* 25.

17. Juliana Claassens, "Commentary on Genesis 22:1-14," Working preacher.org, https://www.workingpreacher.org/preaching.aspx?commentary_id=965.

18. Watts, *The Bible for Children,* 38.

19. Ralph Milton, *The Family Story Bible* (Louisville: Westminster John Knox, 1996), 39–40.

20. Ibid., 40.

21. *Deep Blue Kids Bible,* 25.

22. *Deep Blue Kids Bible,* 1139.

23. Ibid.

24. *Common English Study Bible* (Nashville: CEB, 2013), 109 NT.

25. Ellis, *Candle Read and Share Bible (*Oxford: Candle Books, 2007), 301.

26. Ibid.

27. Levine, *Short Stories by Jesus,* 103–4.

28. Milton, *The Family Story Bible,* 221.

29. Ibid.

30. Owen Edwards, "How Thomas Jefferson Created His Own Bible," *Smithsonian Magazine,* January 2012, www.smithsonianmag.com/arts-culture/how-thomas-jefferson-created-his-own-bible-5659505/.

31. Stephen Prothero, "Thomas Jefferson's Cut-and-Paste Bible," *The Wall Street Journal,* March 25, 2011, http://www.wsj.com/articles/SB10001424052748704425804576220612714039084.

32. Frances Taylor Gench, *Back to the Well: Women's Encounters with Jesus in the Gospels* (Louisville: Westminster John Knox Press, 2004), 48.

33. Watts, *The Bible for Children,* 256.

34. Milton, *The Family Story Bible,* 206.

35. Ellis, *Candle Read and Share,* 333.

36. Watts, *The Bible for Children,* 262.

37. *Shine On: A Story Bible,* 212.

38. Ellis, *Candle Read and Share,* 267.

39. *Deep Blue Kids Bible,* 755.

40. Milton, *The Family Story Bible,* 120.

41. Eva Moore, *American Bible Society Read and Learn Bible* (New York: Scholastic, Inc., 2005), 235.

42. Milton, *Family Story Bible,* 138.

43. Ibid.

44. *Shine On: A Story Bible,* 140.

45. Milton, *Family Story Bible,* 151.

46. Piper, *Lion Read and Know Bible,* 362.

47. Amy Oden, "Commentary on Matthew 5:1-12" *Working Preacher,* February 2, 2014, www.workingpreacher.org/preaching.aspx?commentary_id=1937.

48. Ibid.

49. Ibid.

50. Milton, *Family Story Bible,* 193.

51. Susan Burt, "Nurturing an Imaginative, Inquiring Spirit" in *Faith Forward: A Dialogue on Children, Youth, and a New Kind of Christianity,* vol. 1, eds. David M. Csinos and Melvin Bray (Kelowna, BC: CopperHouse, 2013), 121.

52. This line is from the third verse of the hymn, "My Shepherd Will Supply My Need" by Isaac Watts, 1719.

5. How We Support Families with Children

Epigraph: Melody Briggs, "The Word Became Visual Text: The Boy Jesus in Children's Bibles" in *Text, Image and Otherness in Children's Bibles: What Is in the Picture?,* eds. Caroline Vander Stichele and Hugh S. Pyper (Atlanta: Society of Biblical Literature, 2012), 170.

1. Tom Long uses this phrase in his excellent description of an exegesis for preaching in *The Witness of Preaching* (Louisville: Westminster John Knox Press, 1999), 68.

2. Susan Burt, "Nurturing an Imaginative, Inquiring Spirit" in *Faith Forward,* 122–23.

3. These ideas have come from the suggestions of Jim Burke, "103 Things to Do Before/During/After Reading," *Reading Rockets,* http://www.readingrockets.org/article/103-things-do-beforeduringafter-reading.

CPSIA information can be obtained at www.ICGtesting.com
Printed in the USA
LVOW11s0110060516

486745LV00003B/6/P